About the book:

Kids coloring books are interactive activity books designed specifically for children to engage in creative and artistic expression. These books typically feature various line drawings or illustrations of animals, characters, objects, and scenes that are suitable for coloring.

Animal-themed kids coloring books specifically focus on presenting a wide range of animals, including mammals, birds, reptiles, amphibians, and marine creatures. The illustrations depict these animals in a simplified and kid-friendly style, allowing children to easily identify and color them.

The coloring book pages often contain bold outlines and large spaces, making it easier for young children to color within the lines. This helps develop their fine motor skills, hand-eye coordination, and concentration.

Besides providing enjoyment and entertainment, kids coloring books offer several benefits for children's development. They encourage creativity, imagination, and self-expression, as children can choose their own colors and bring the illustrations to life in their unique way. Coloring also promotes relaxation, mindfulness, and a sense of accomplishment, as children complete each page.

Content:

1 - Cat
2 - Octopus
3 - Snake
4 - Dog

5 - Fish
6 - Bear
7 - Landscape

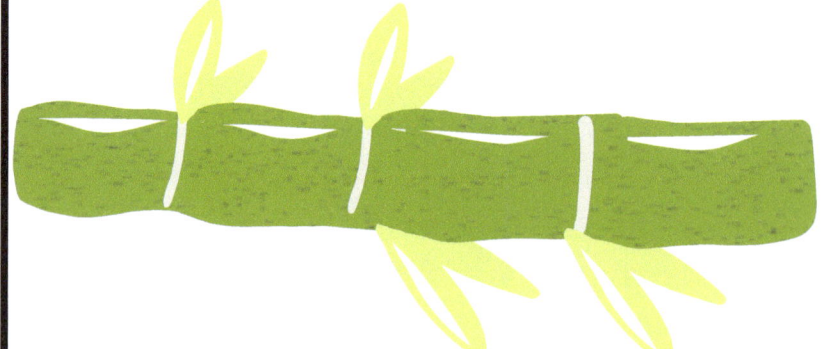

SUMMARIZING TABLE

STEPS TO FOLLOW WHEN PAINTING A SKETCH OF A CAT

Step	Description
1	Gather your materials: sketching paper, pencils, eraser, paints, and brushes.
2	Choose a reference image of a cat.
3	Start with a rough sketch, outlining basic shapes and proportions.
4	Add details such as facial features, ears, eyes, and tail.
5	Refine the sketch, erasing unnecessary lines and making adjustments.
6	Choose your painting technique (e.g., watercolours, acrylics).
7	Begin painting, starting with the background or larger areas of colour.
8	Add depth and shadows with darker shades or mix in black or brown.
9	Fine-tune the details, adding intricate features like fur strands and whiskers.
10	Make any final adjustments or touch-ups. Sign your artwork if desired.

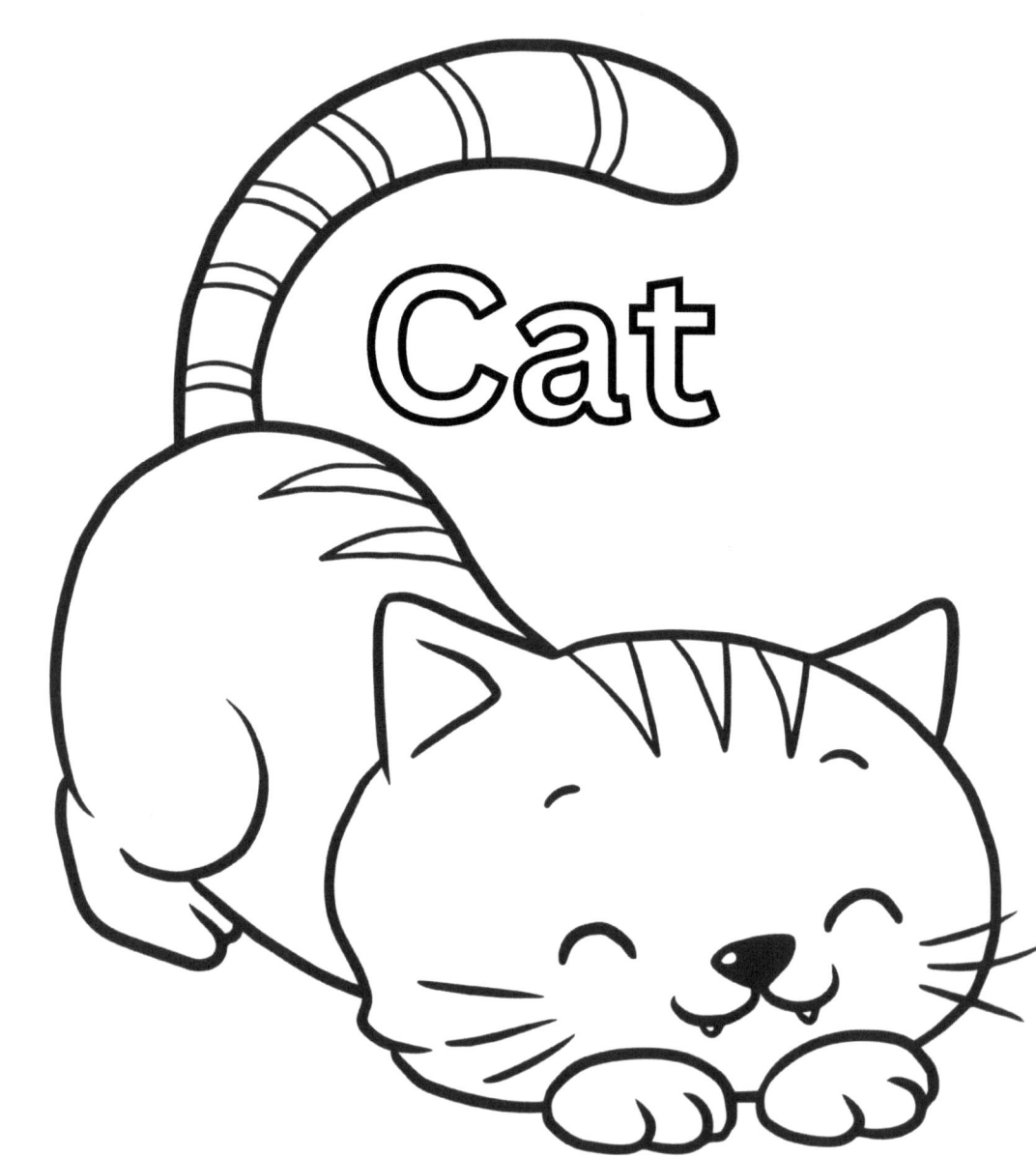

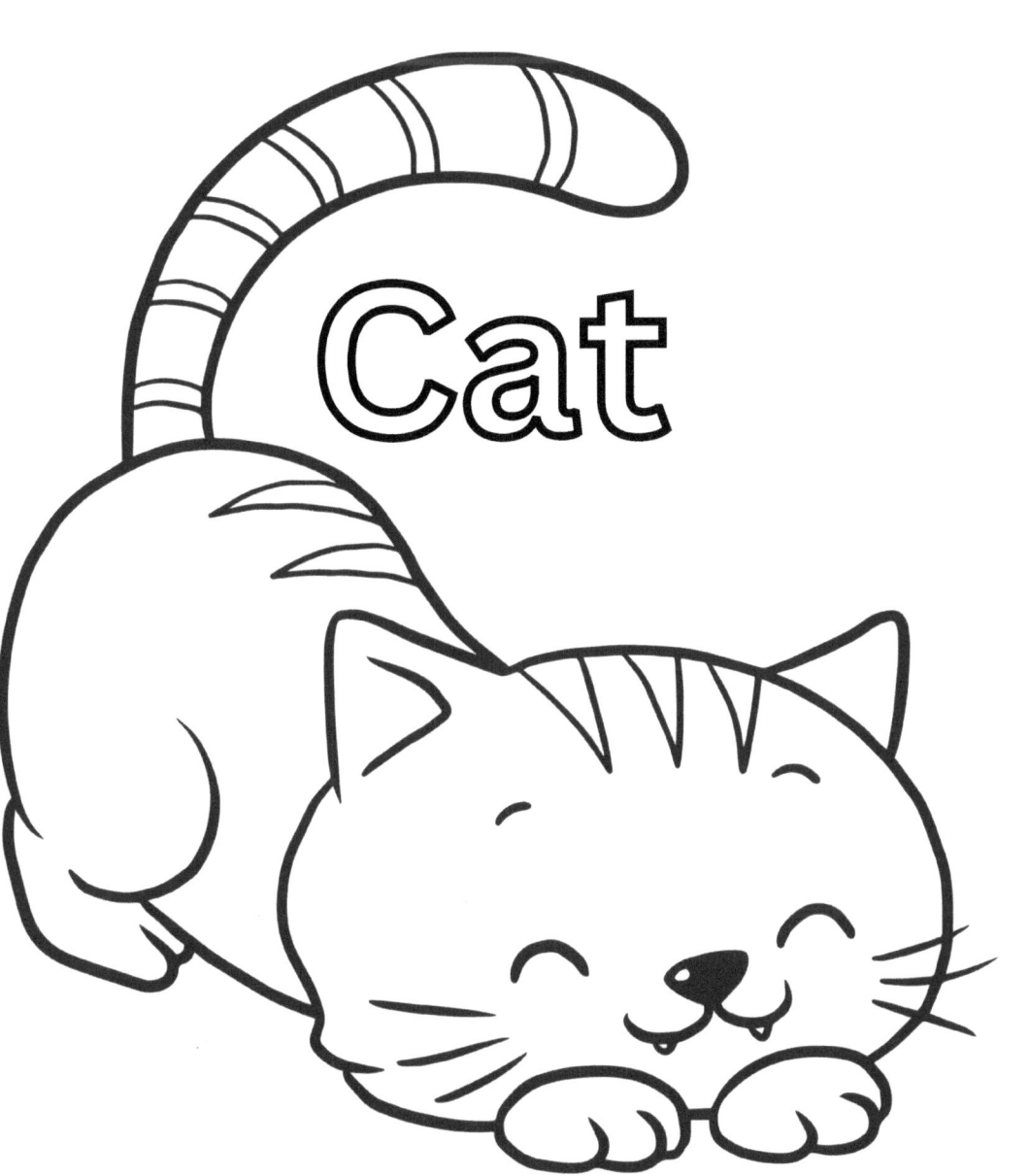

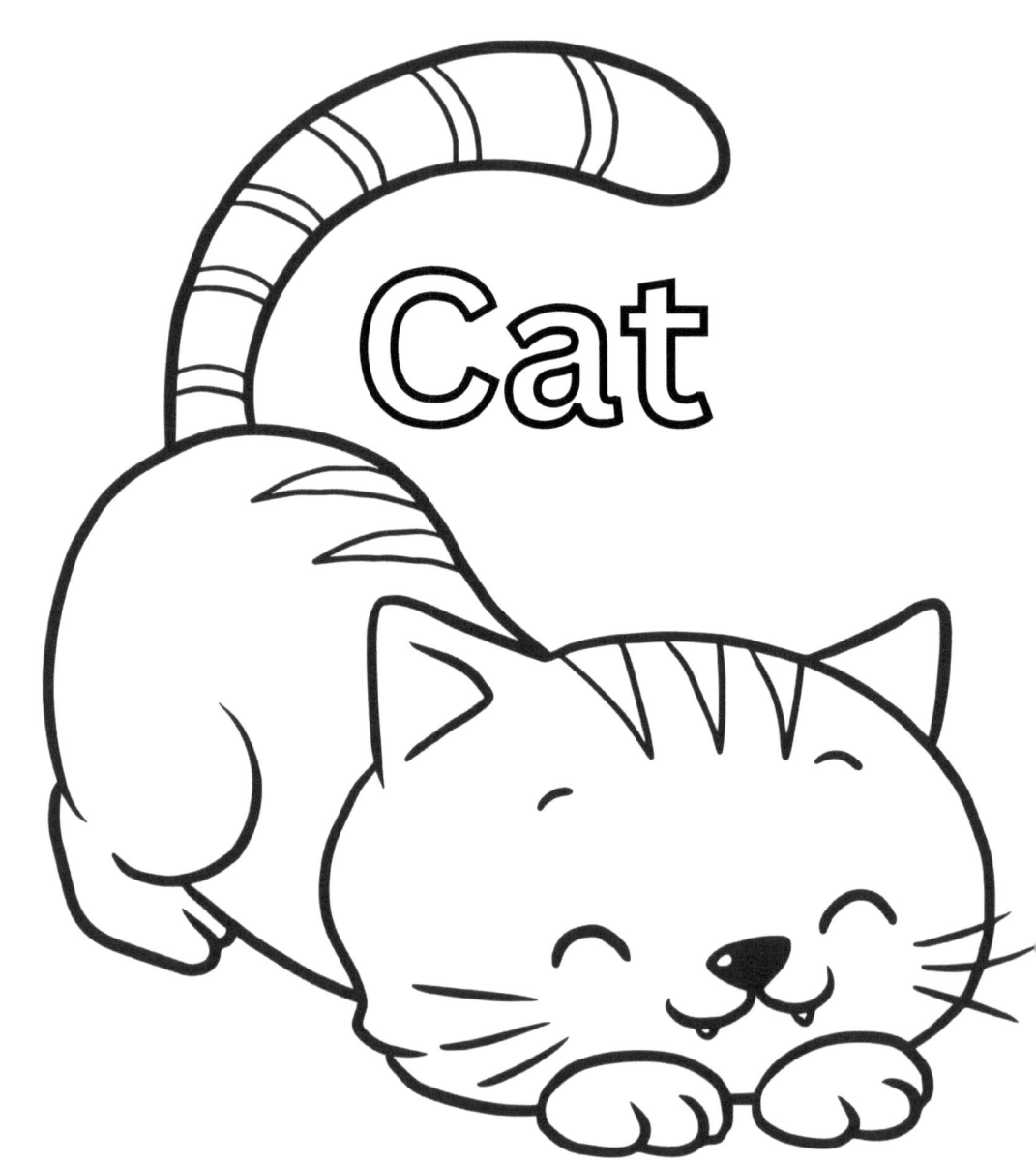

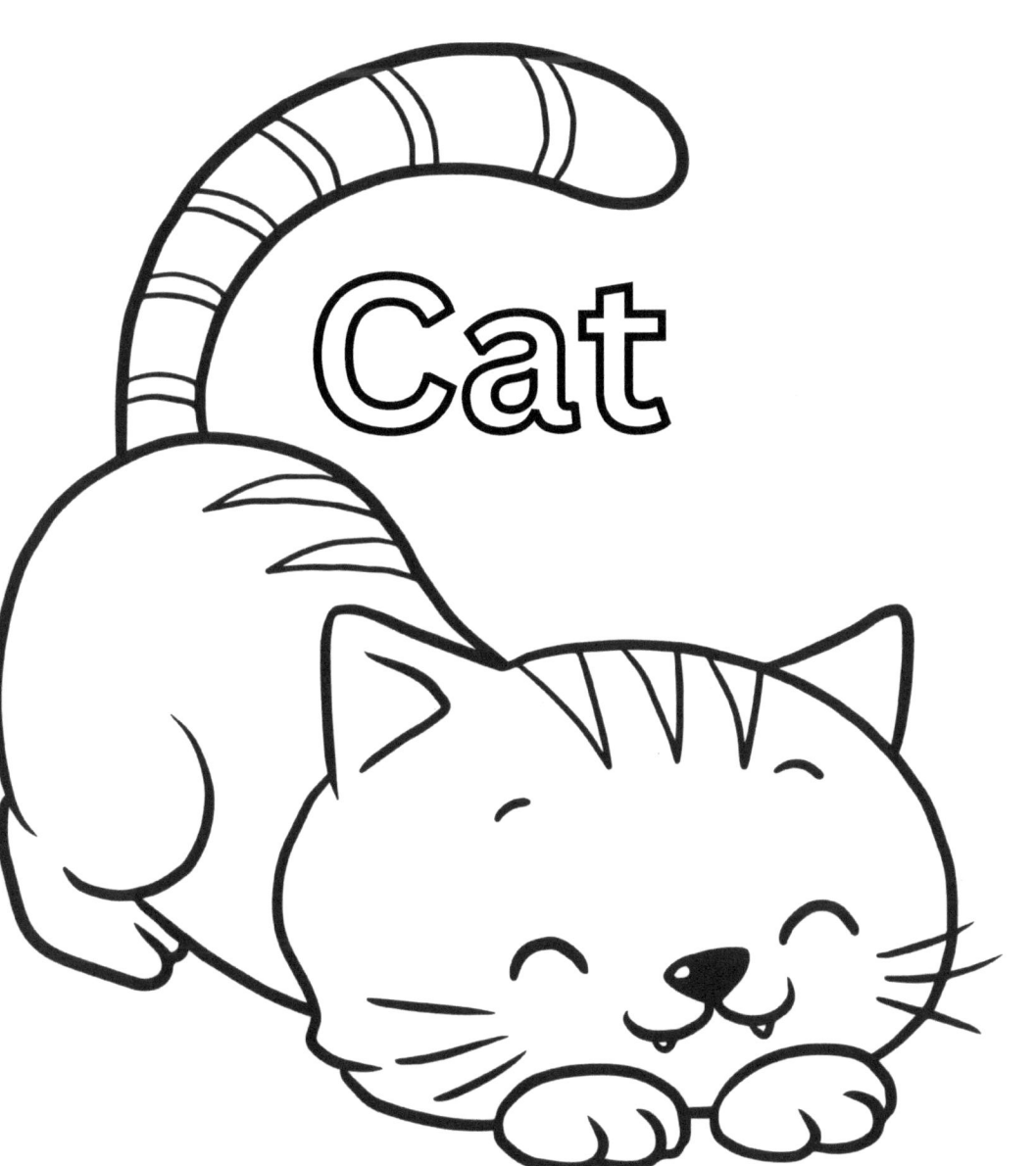

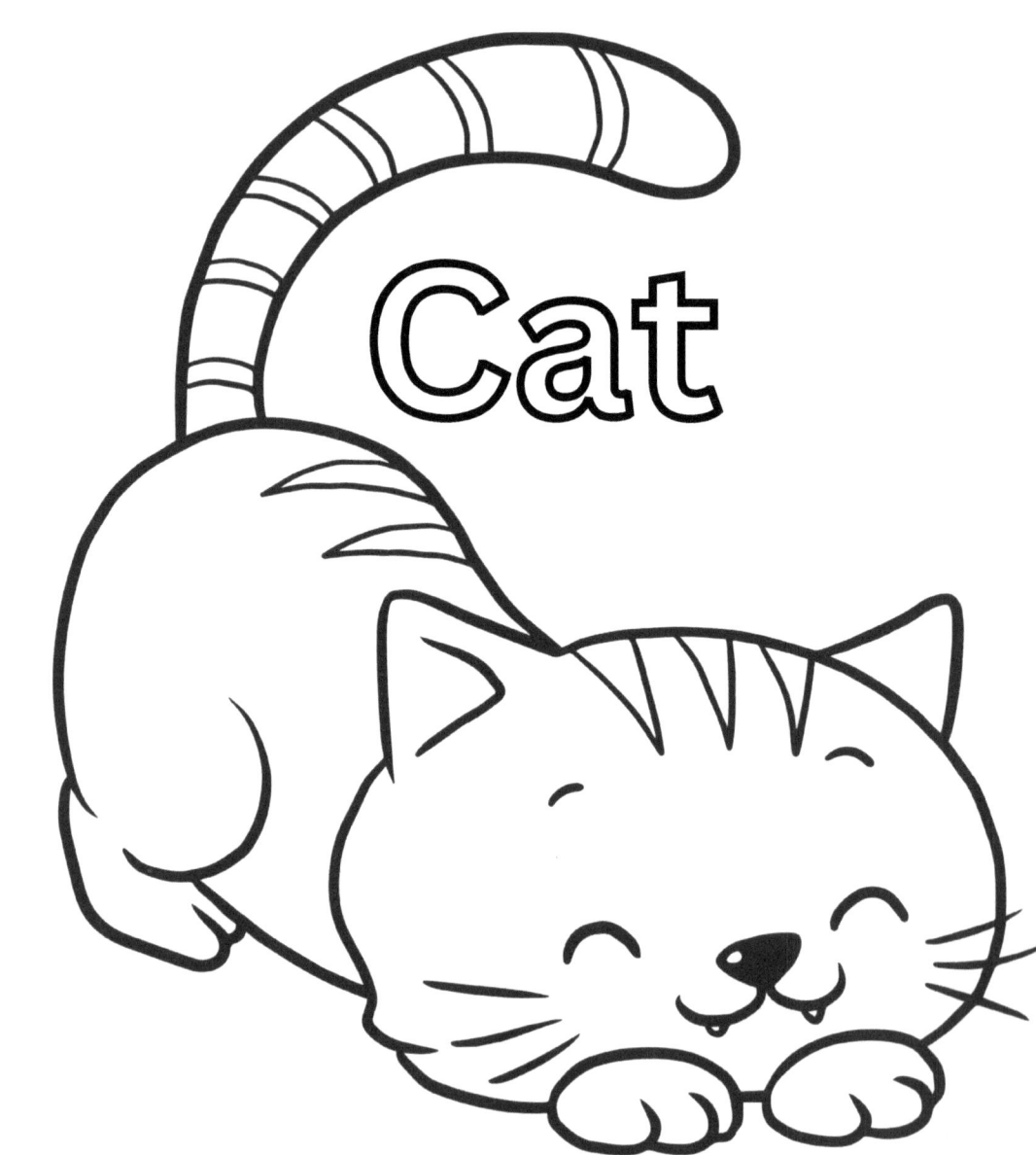

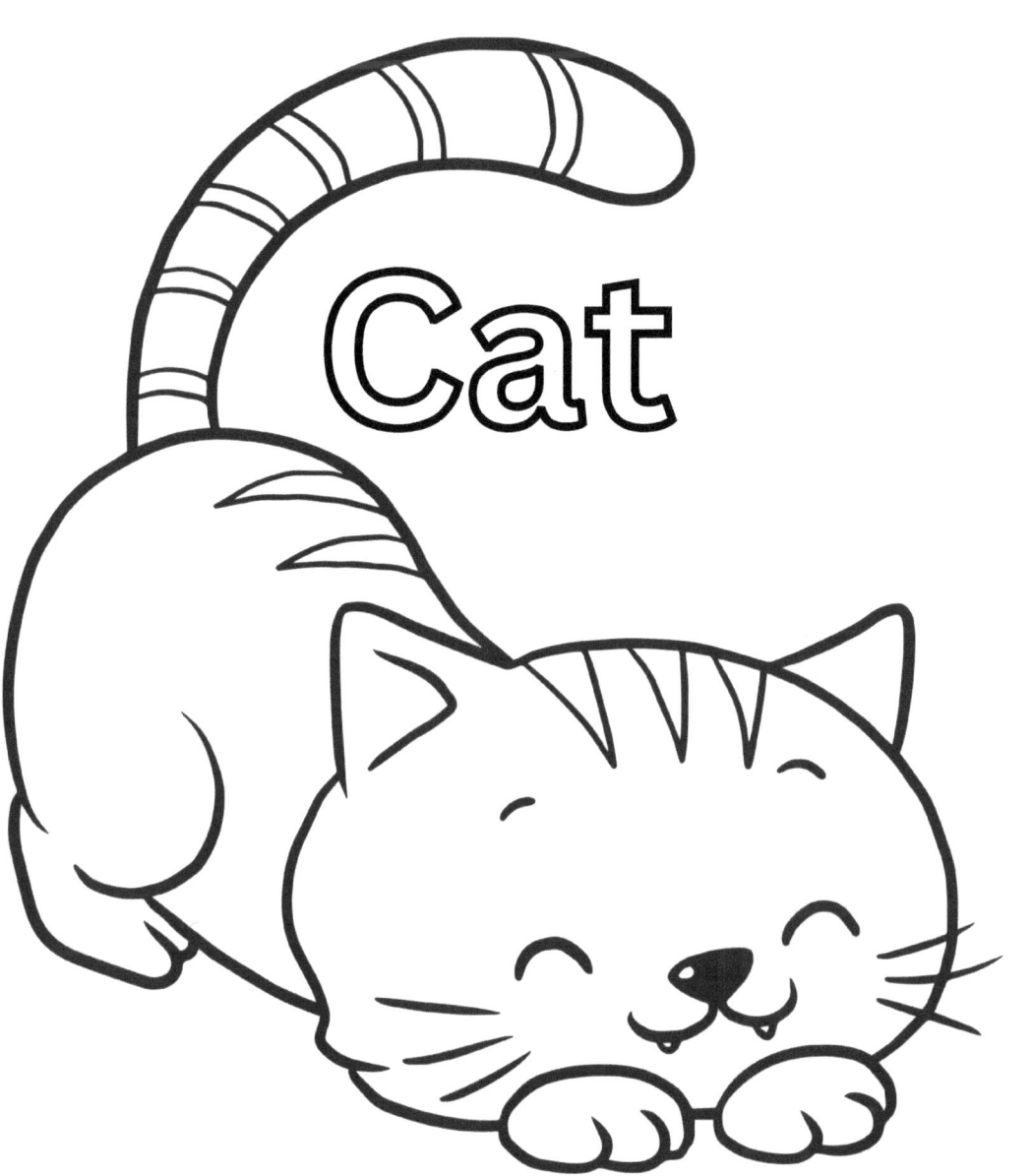

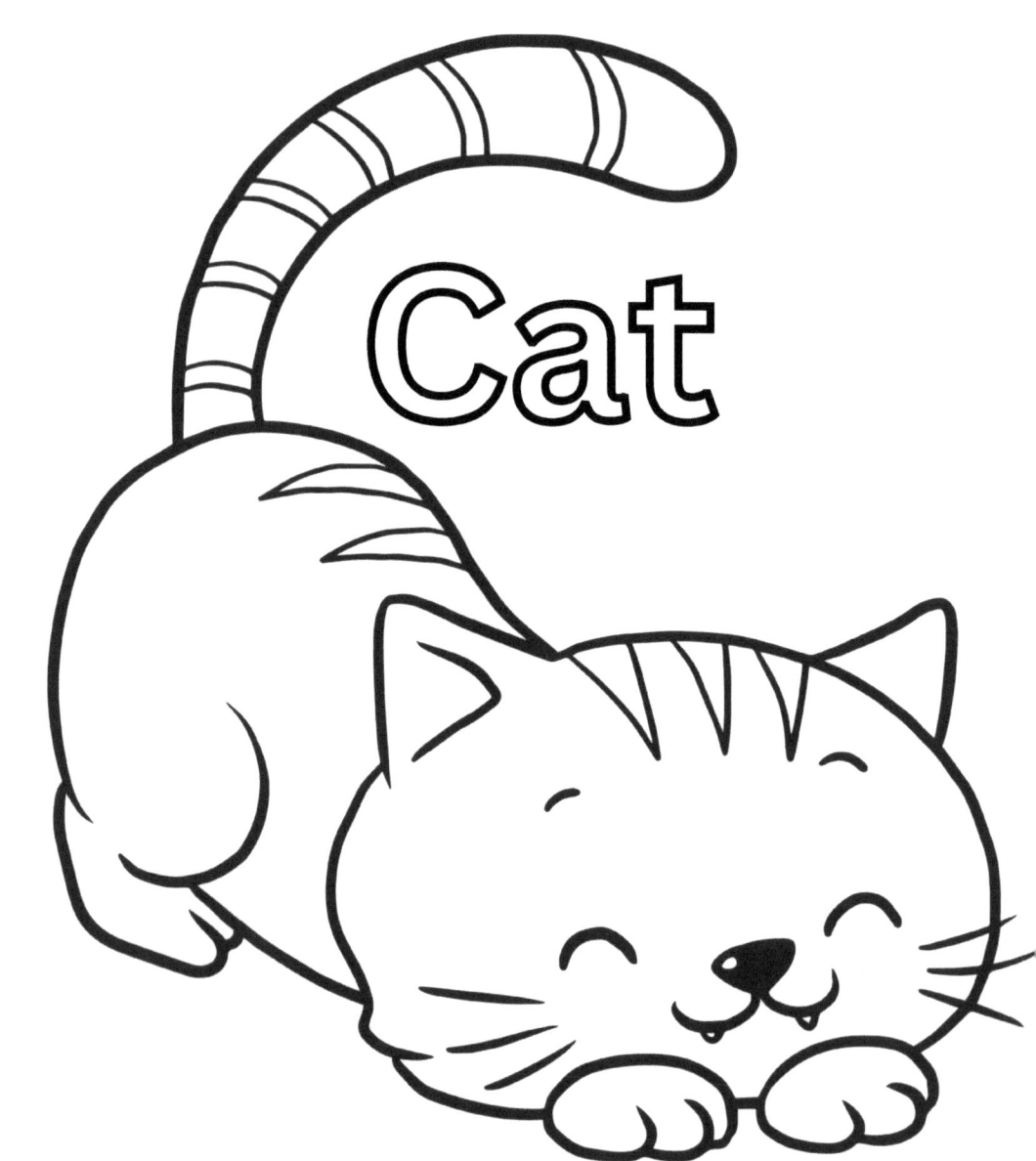

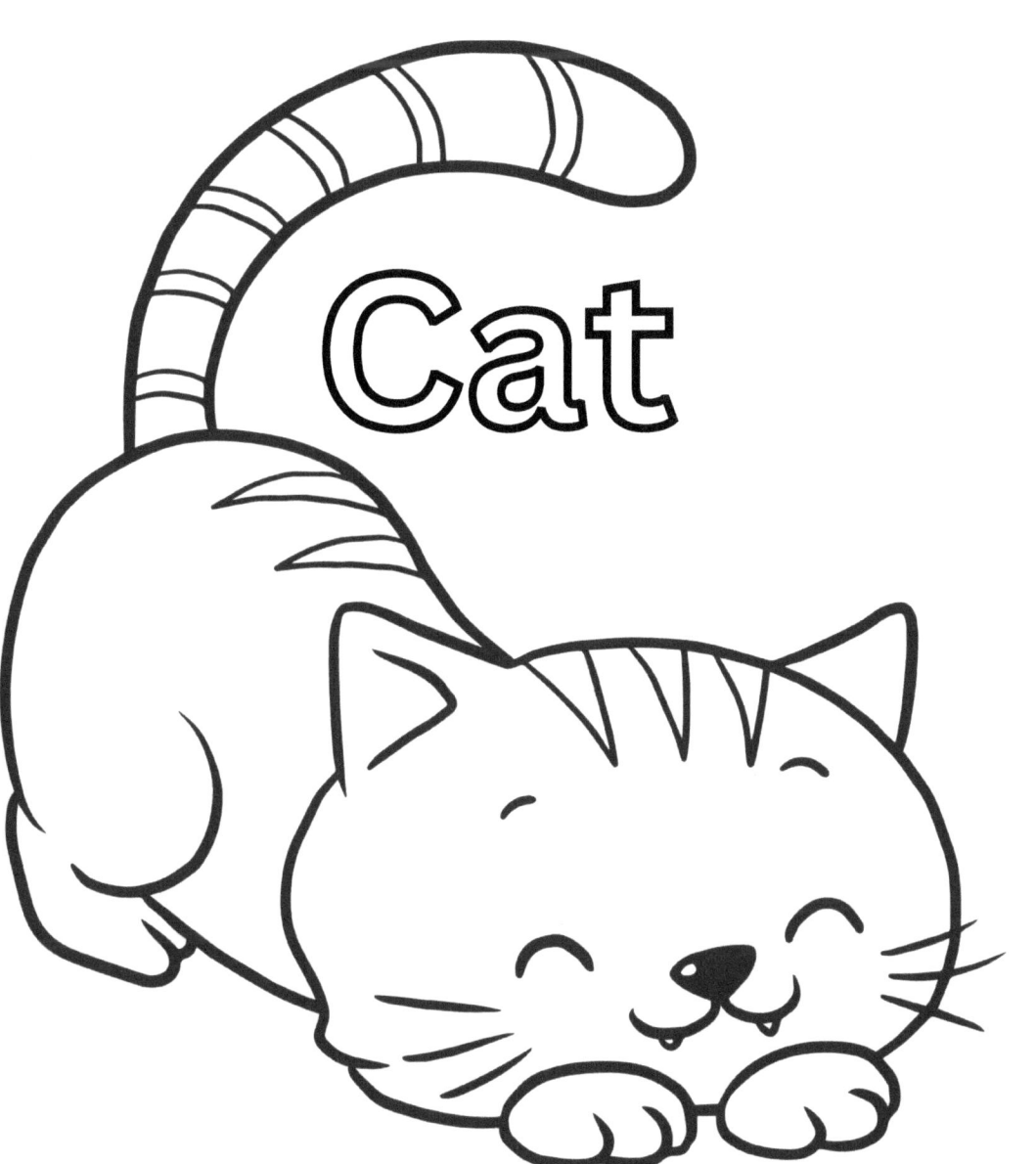

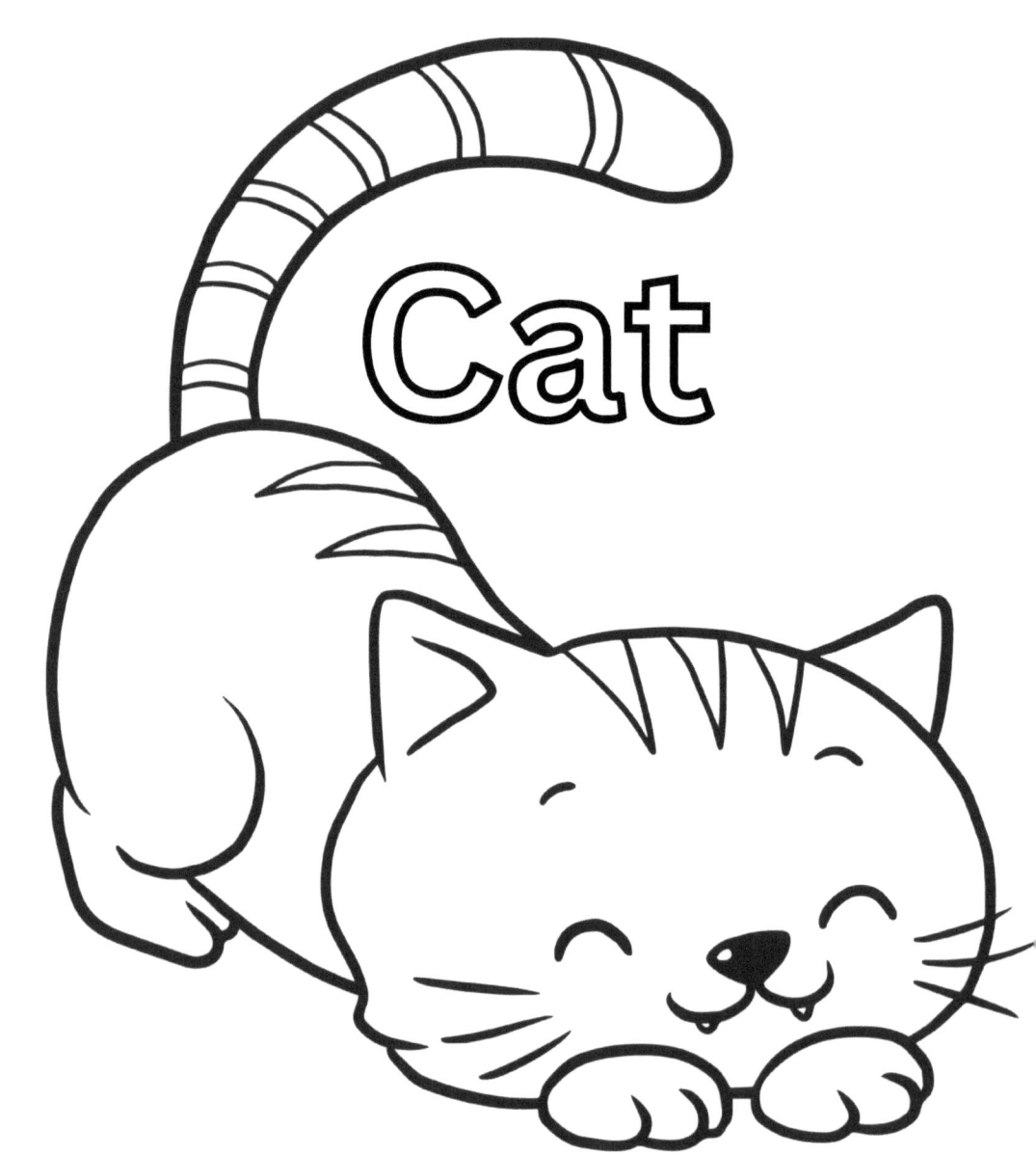

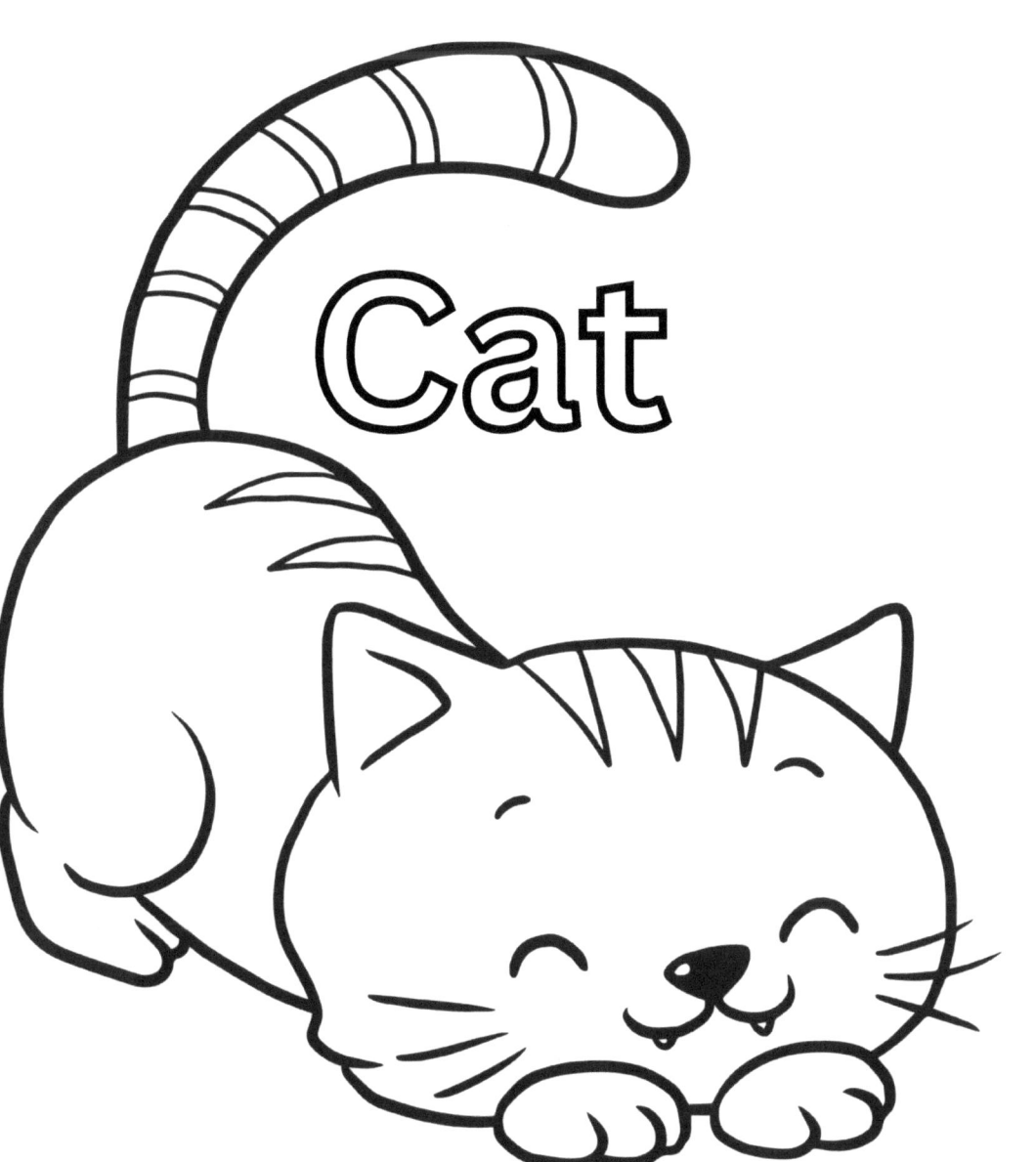

TABLE SUMMARIZING
STEPS TO FOLLOW WHEN PAINTING A SKETCH OF AN OCTOPUS:

Step	Description
1	Gather your materials: sketching paper, pencils, eraser, paints, and brushes.
2	Choose a reference image of an octopus.
3	Start with a rough sketch, outlining the basic shape of the octopus's body.
4	Add details such as the octopus's tentacles and head.
5	Refine the sketch, erasing unnecessary lines and making adjustments.
6	Choose your painting technique (e.g., watercolours, acrylics).
7	Begin painting, starting with the background or larger areas of colour.
8	Add depth and shadows with darker shades or mix in black or brown.
9	Fine-tune the details, adding texture and suction cups to the octopus's body.
10	Make any final adjustments or touch-ups. Sign your artwork if desired.

Octopus

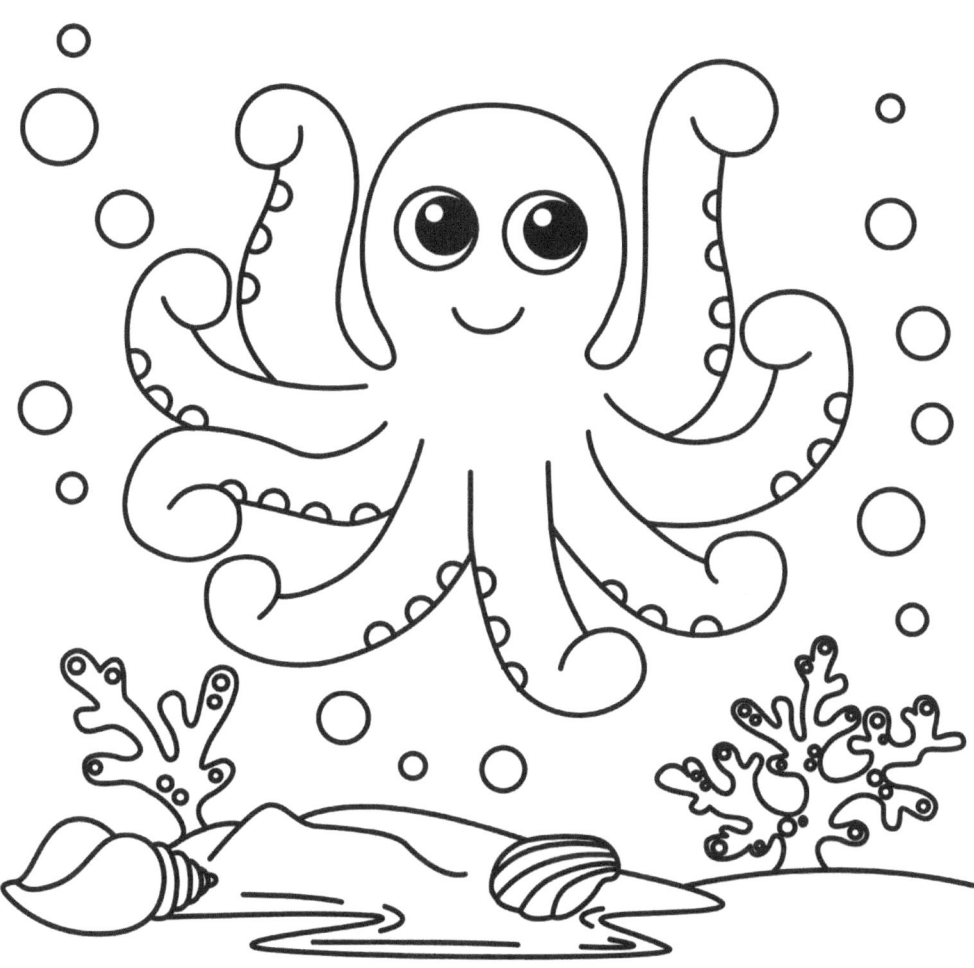

Octopus

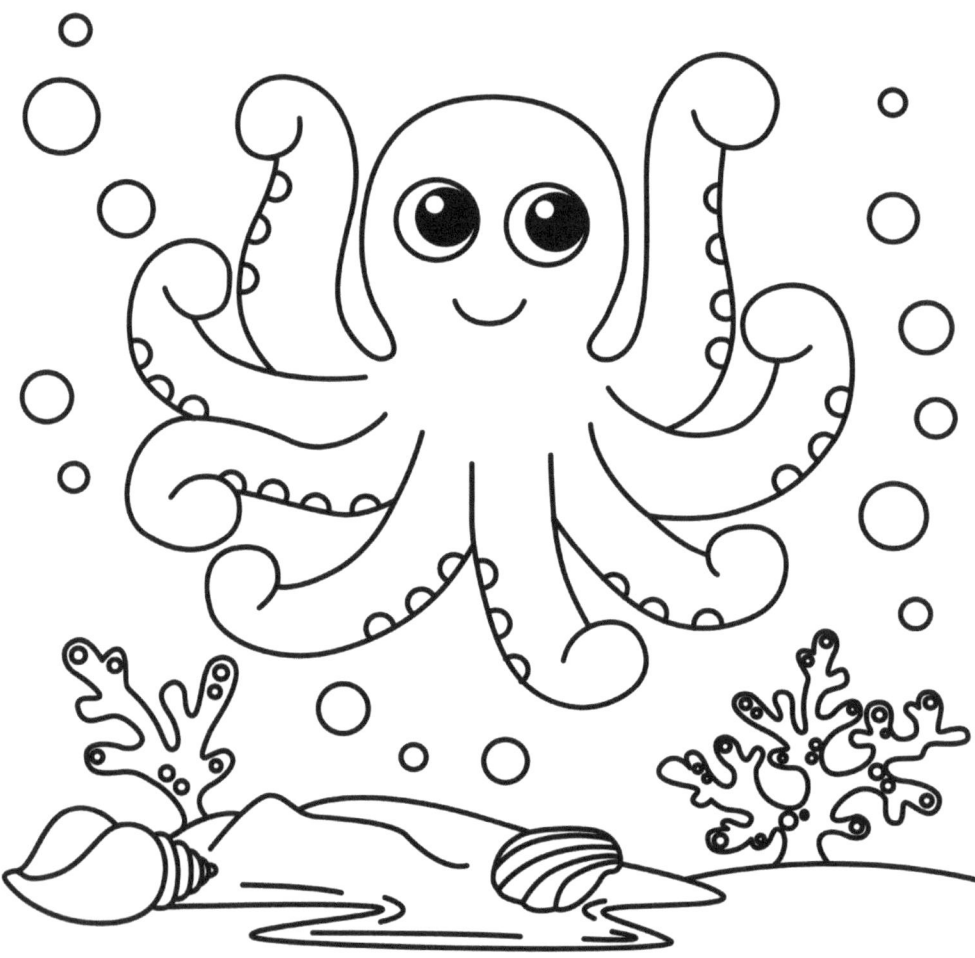

Octopus

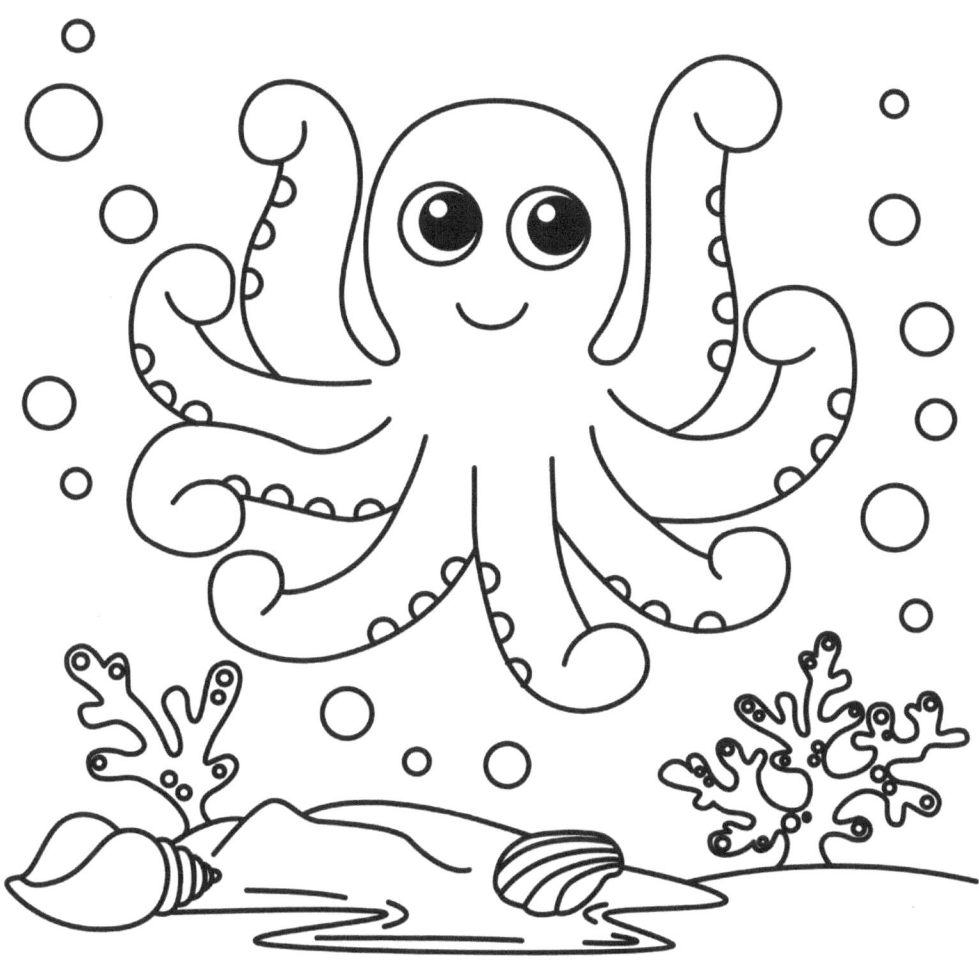

Octopus

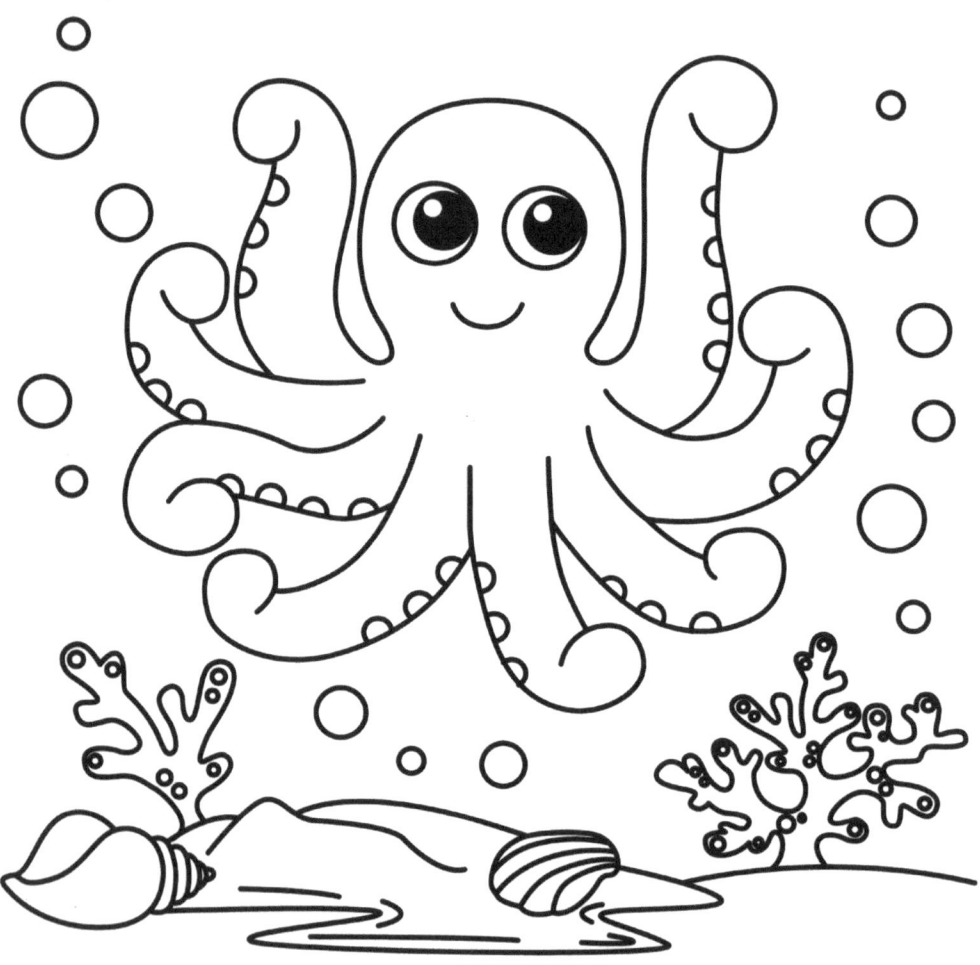

Octopus

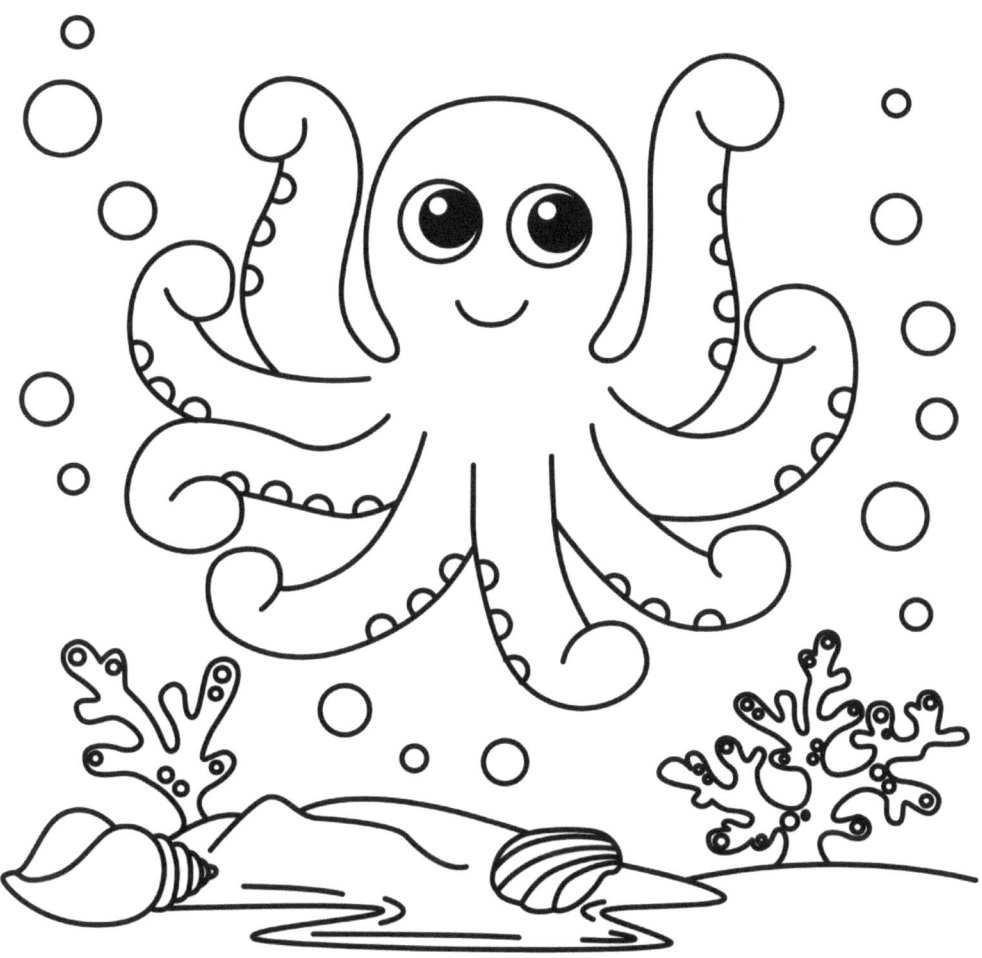

Octopus

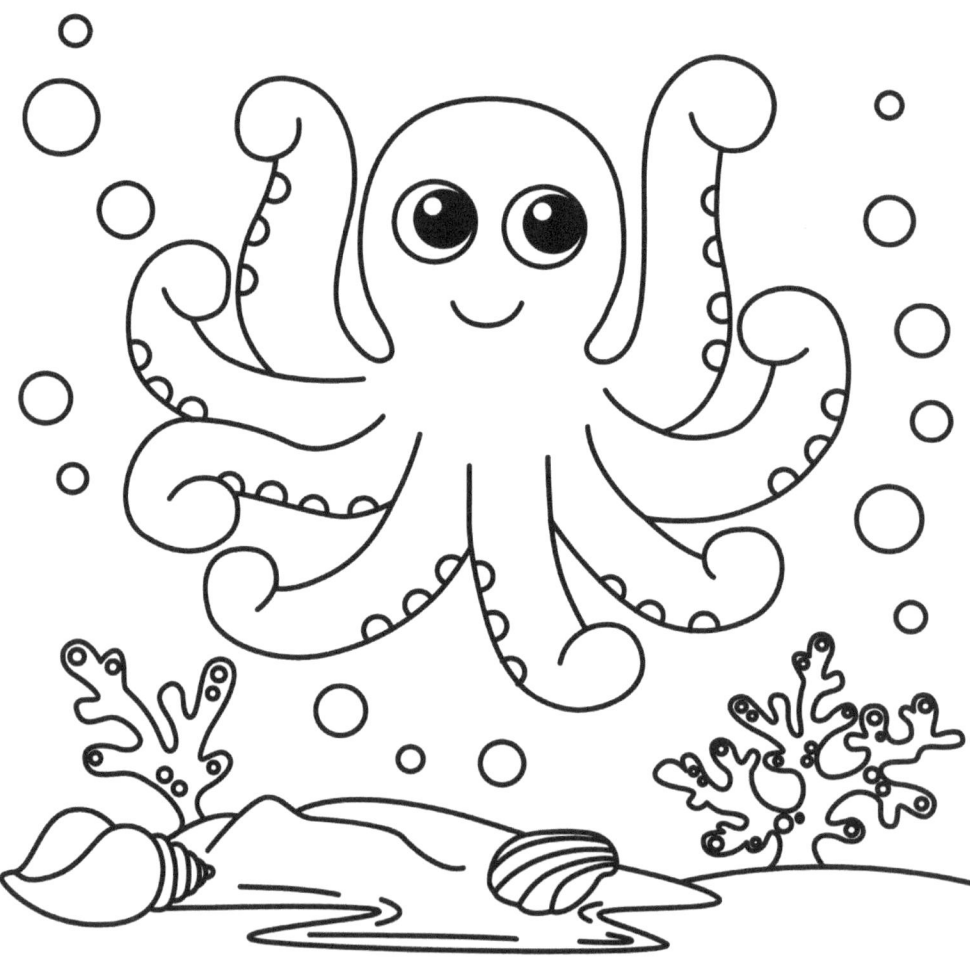

Octopus

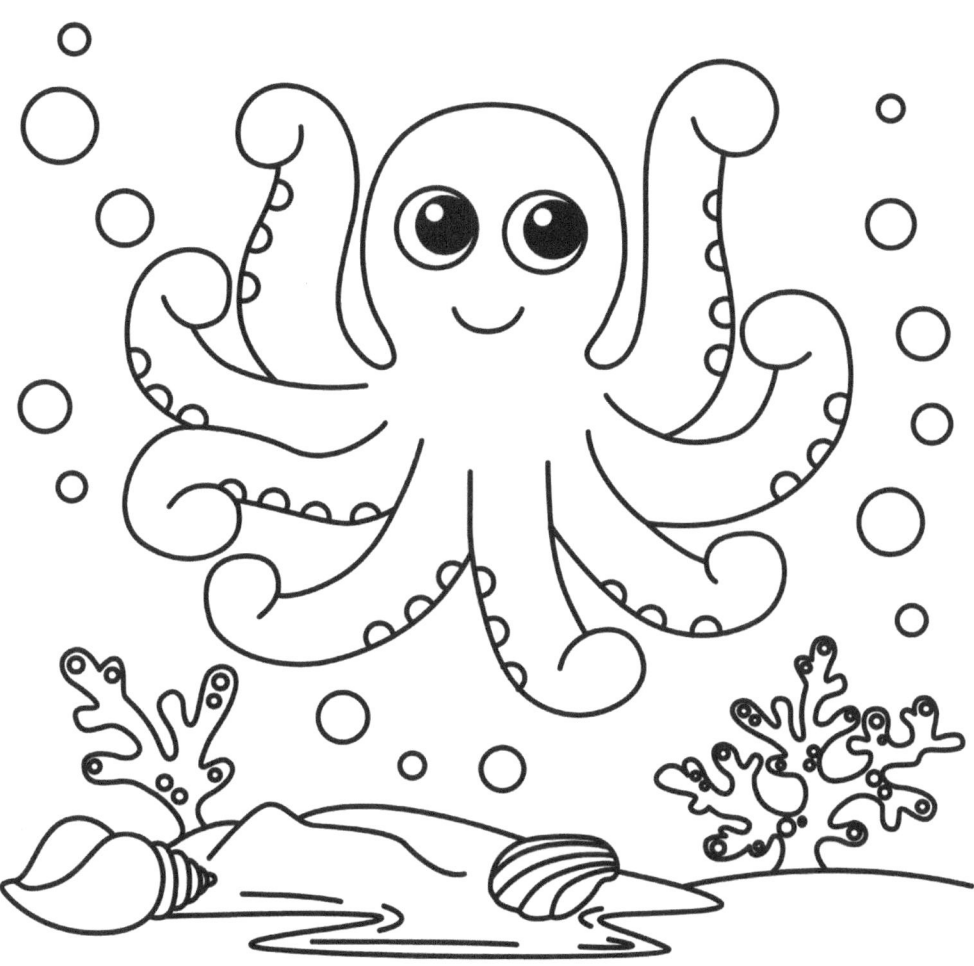

Octopus

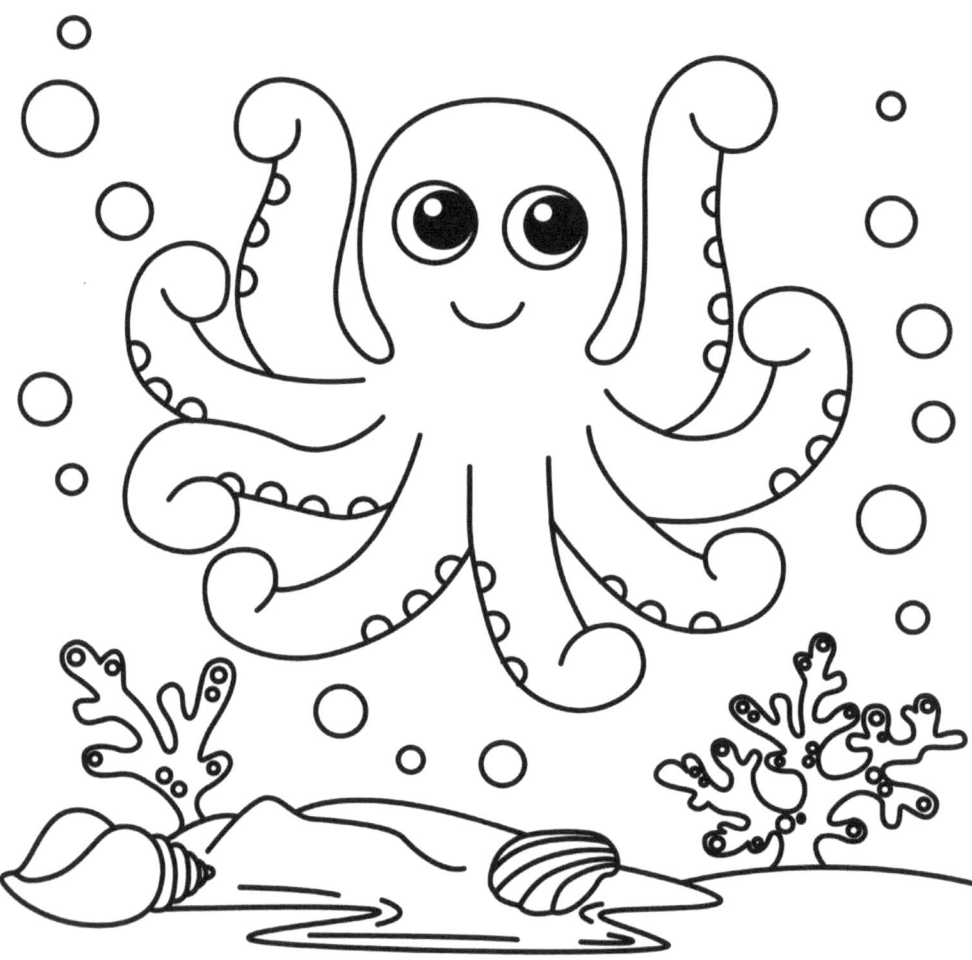

Octopus

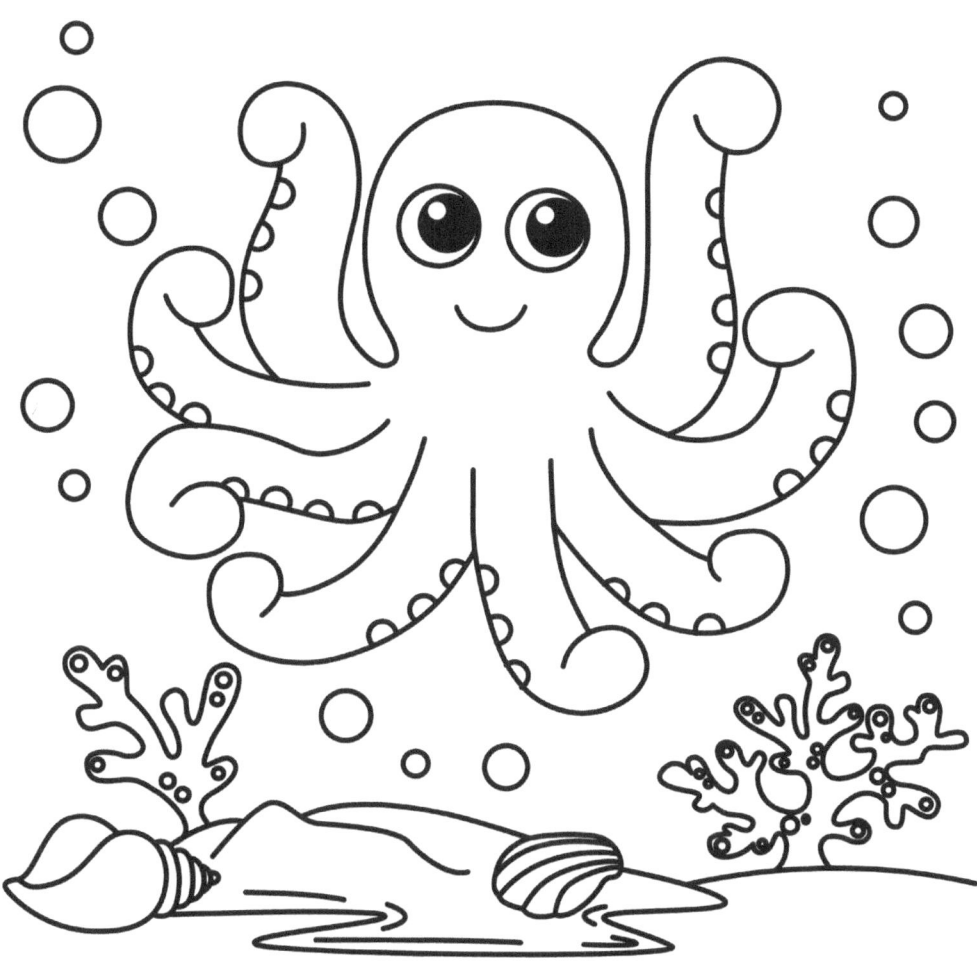

Octopus

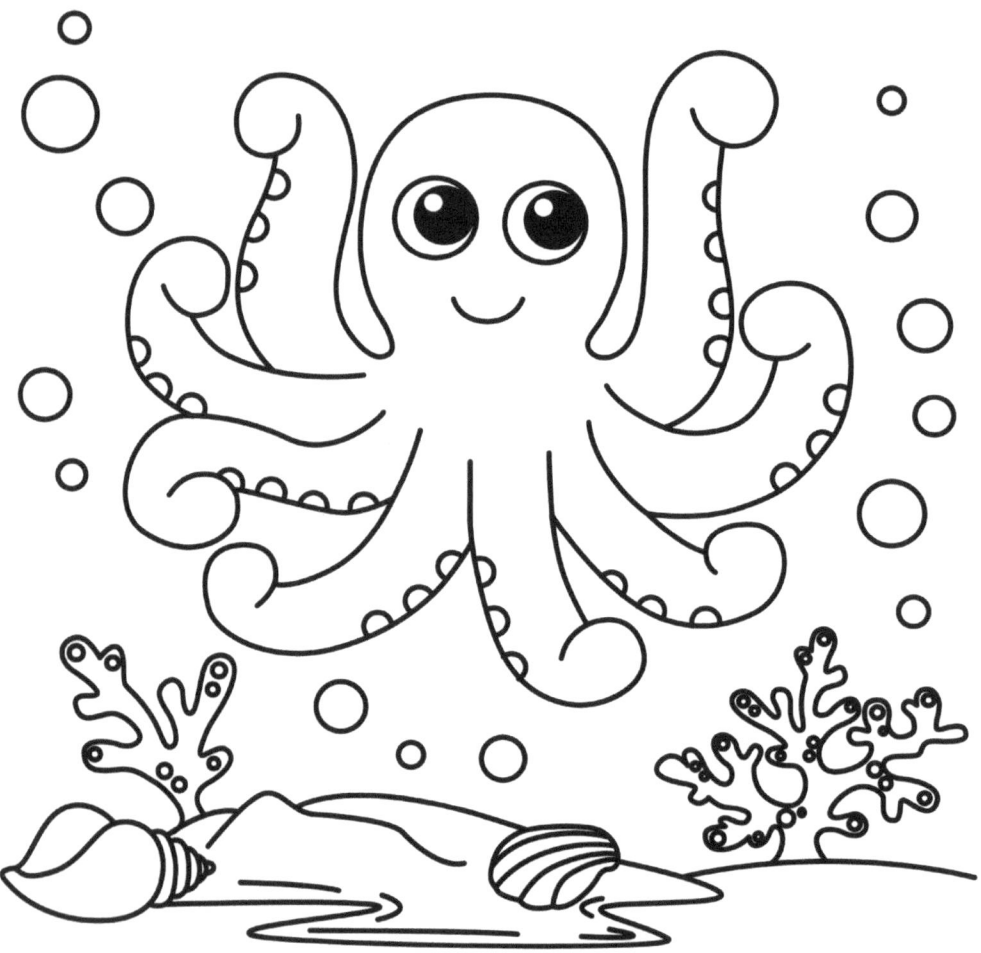

TABLE SUMMARIZING
STEPS TO FOLLOW WHEN PAINTING A SKETCH OF A SNAKE

Step	Description
1	Gather your materials: sketching paper, pencils, eraser, paints, and brushes.
2	Choose a reference image of a snake.
3	Start with a rough sketch, outlining the basic shape of the snake's body.
4	Add details such as the snake's head, eyes, and mouth.
5	Refine the sketch, erasing unnecessary lines and making adjustments.
6	Choose your painting technique (e.g., watercolours, acrylics).
7	Begin painting, starting with the background or larger areas of colour.
8	Add depth and shadows with darker shades or mix in black or brown.
9	Fine-tune the details, adding texture and scales to the snake's body.
10	Make any final adjustments or touch-ups. Sign your artwork if desired.

Snake

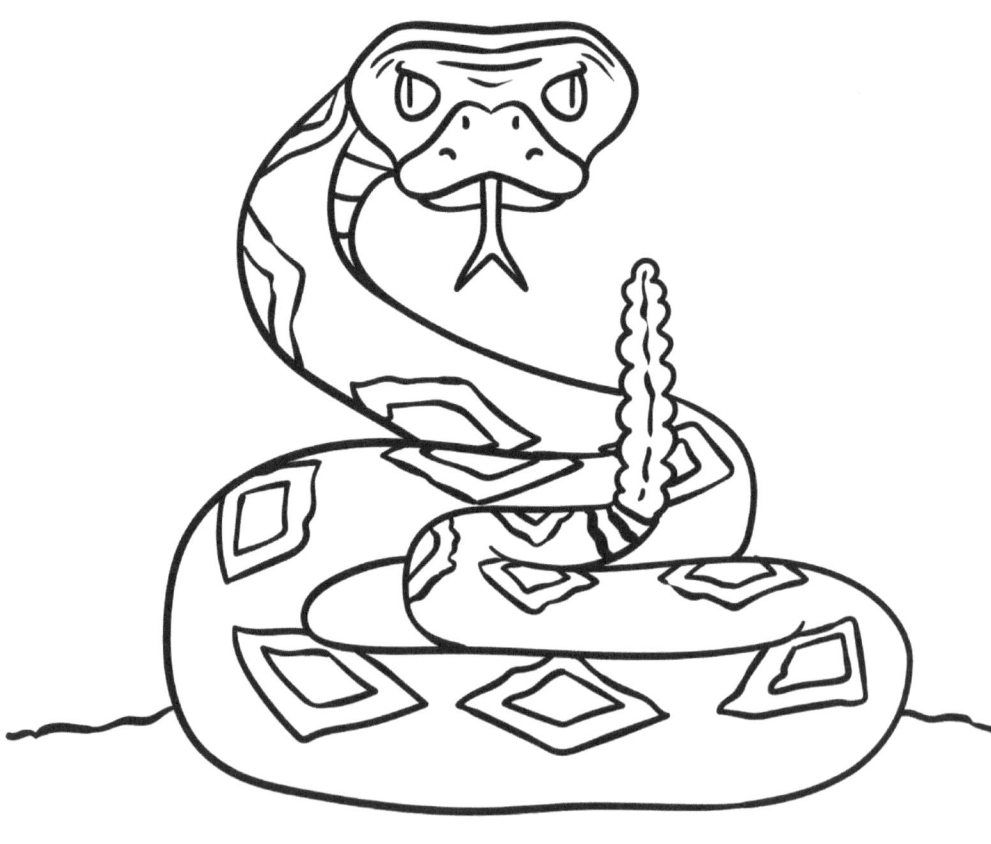

Snake

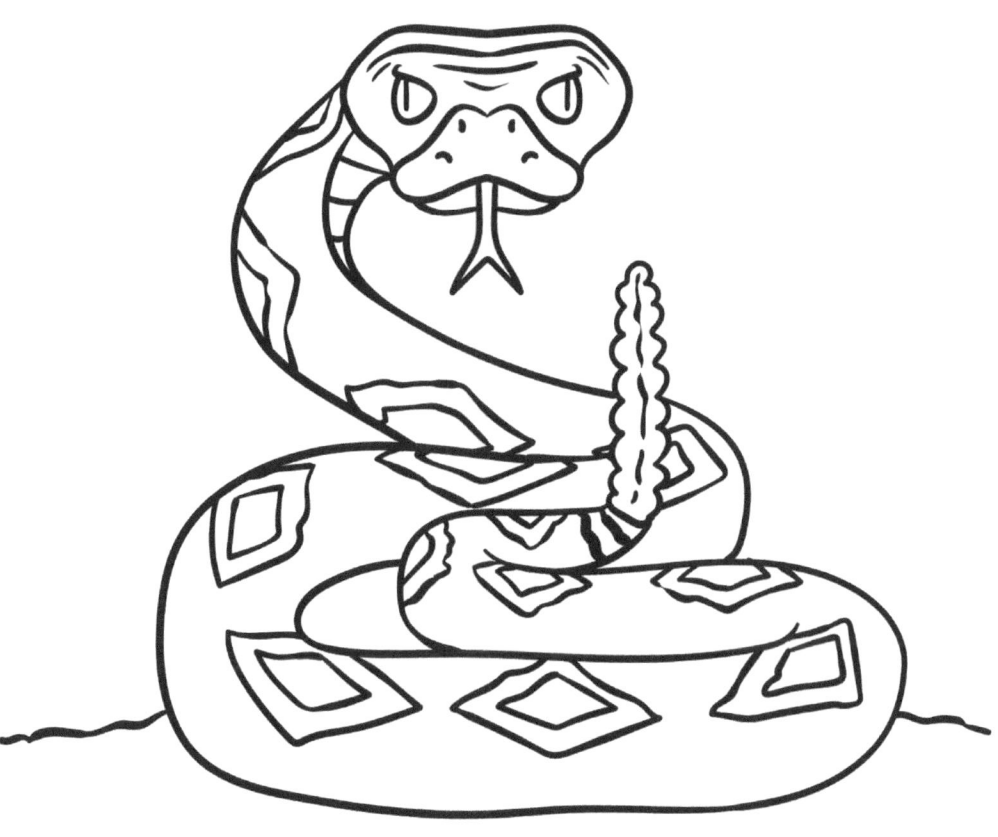

Snake

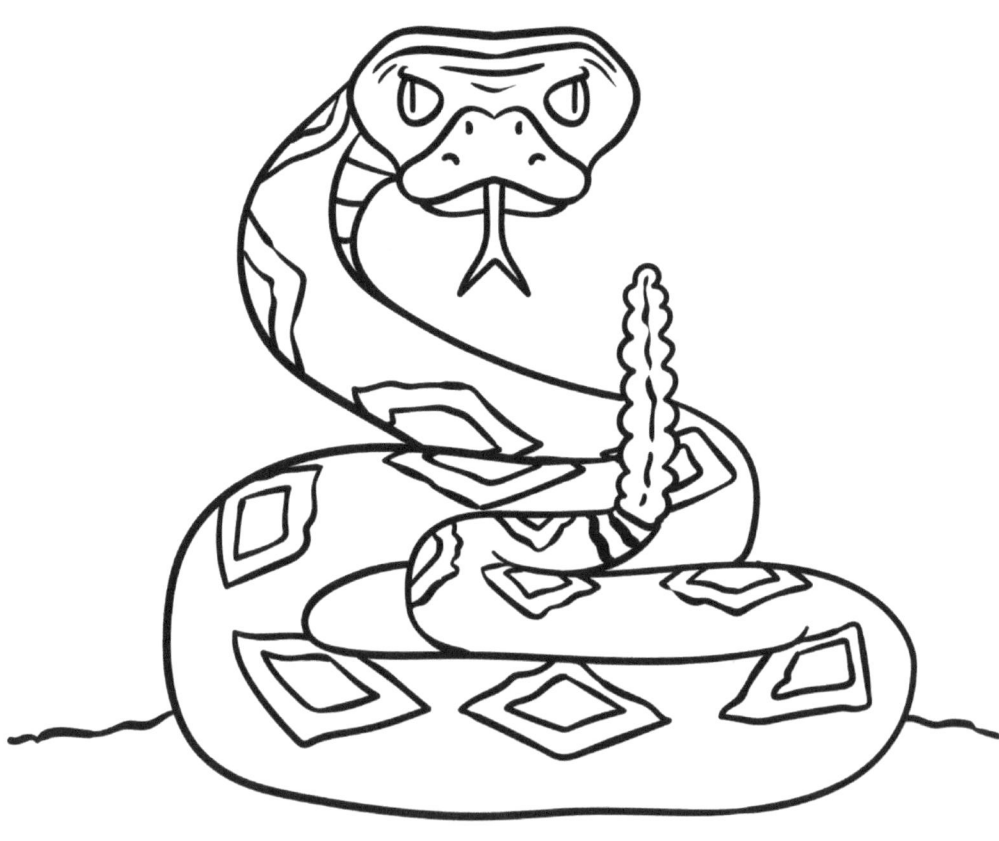

Snake

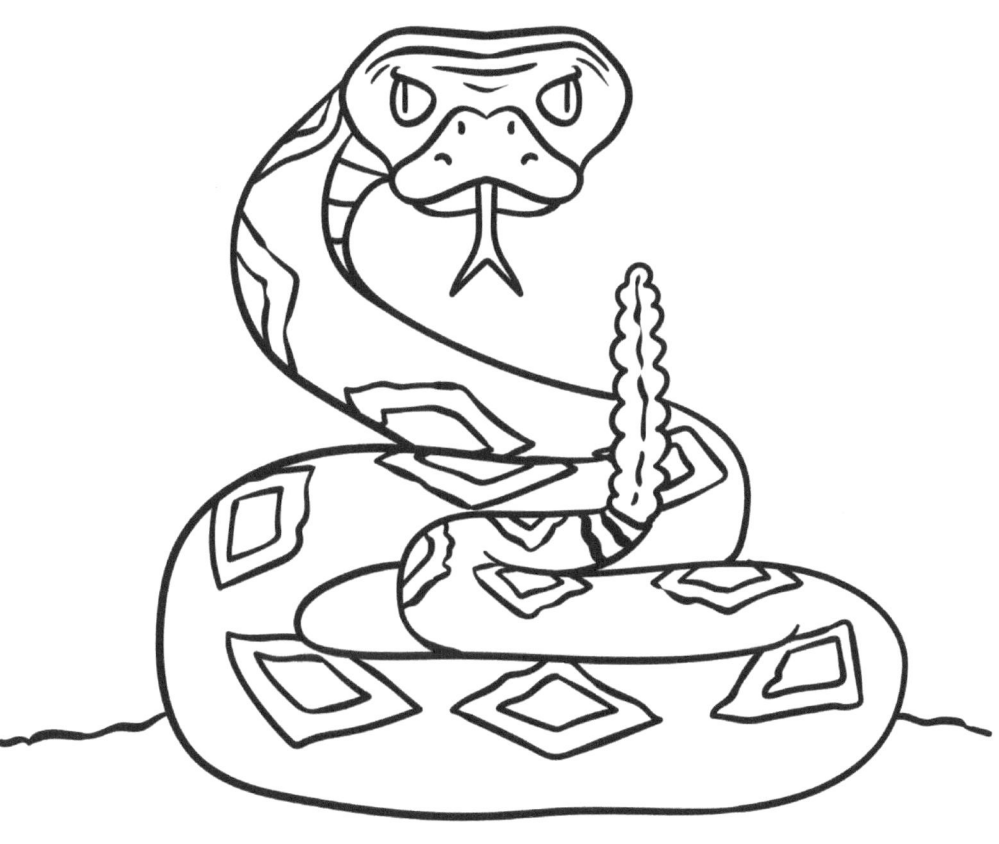

Snake

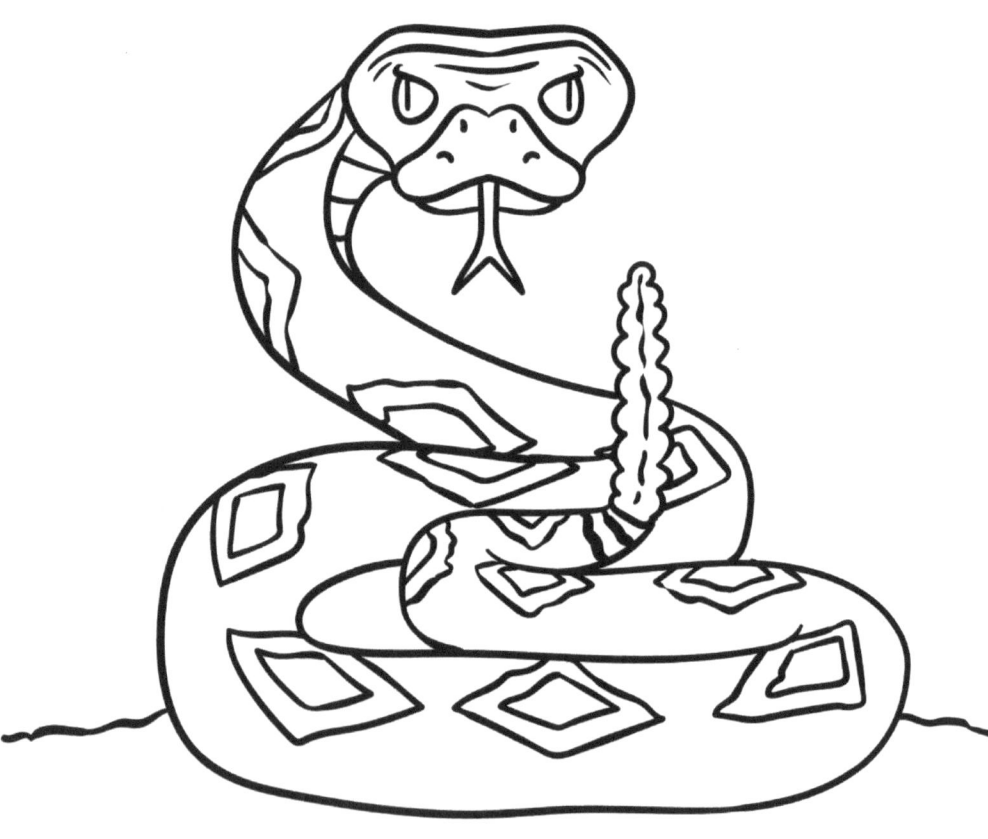

Snake

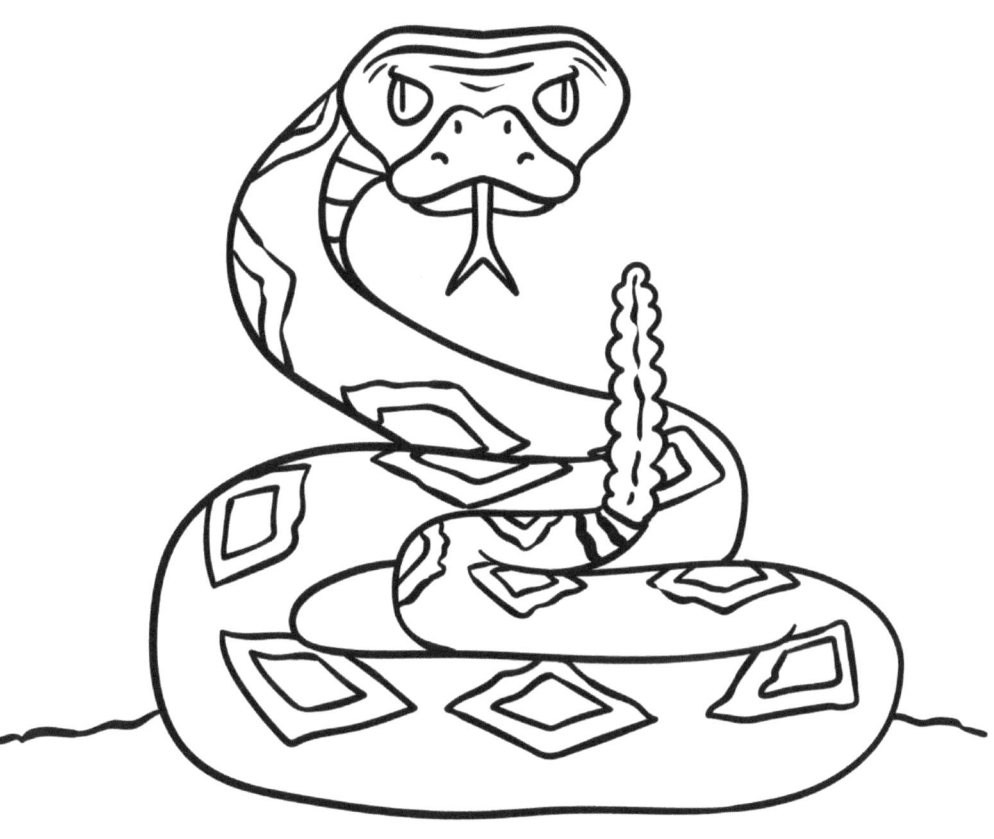

Snake

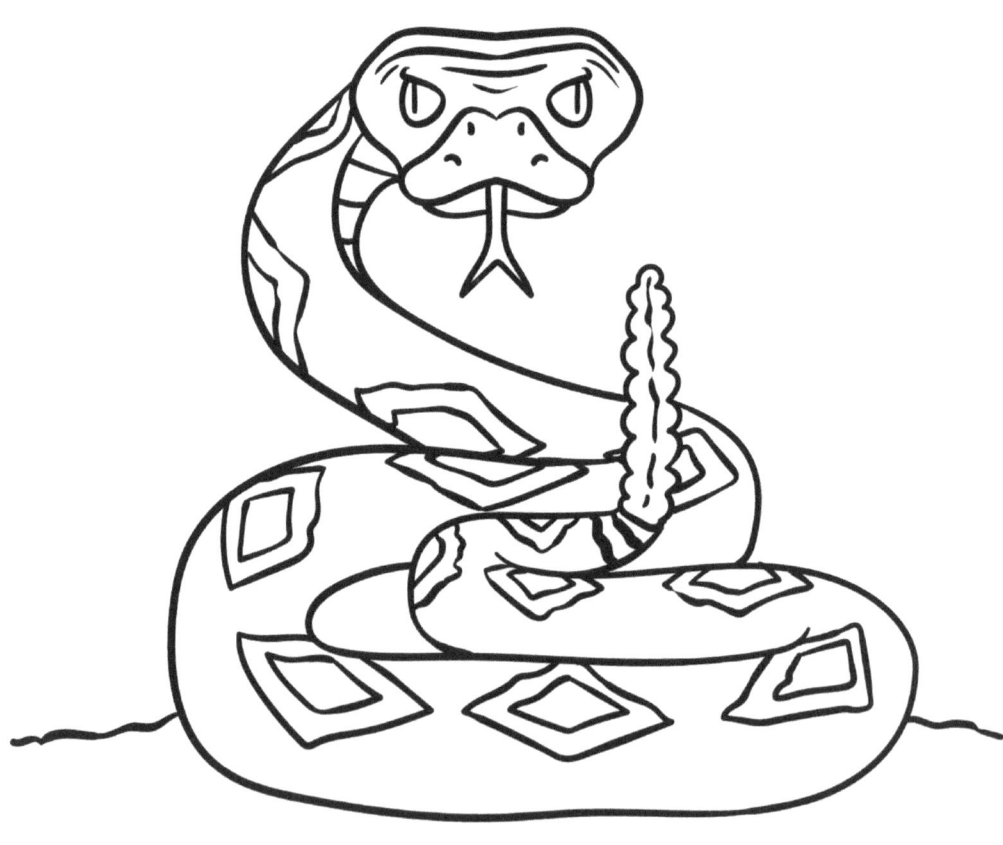

Snake

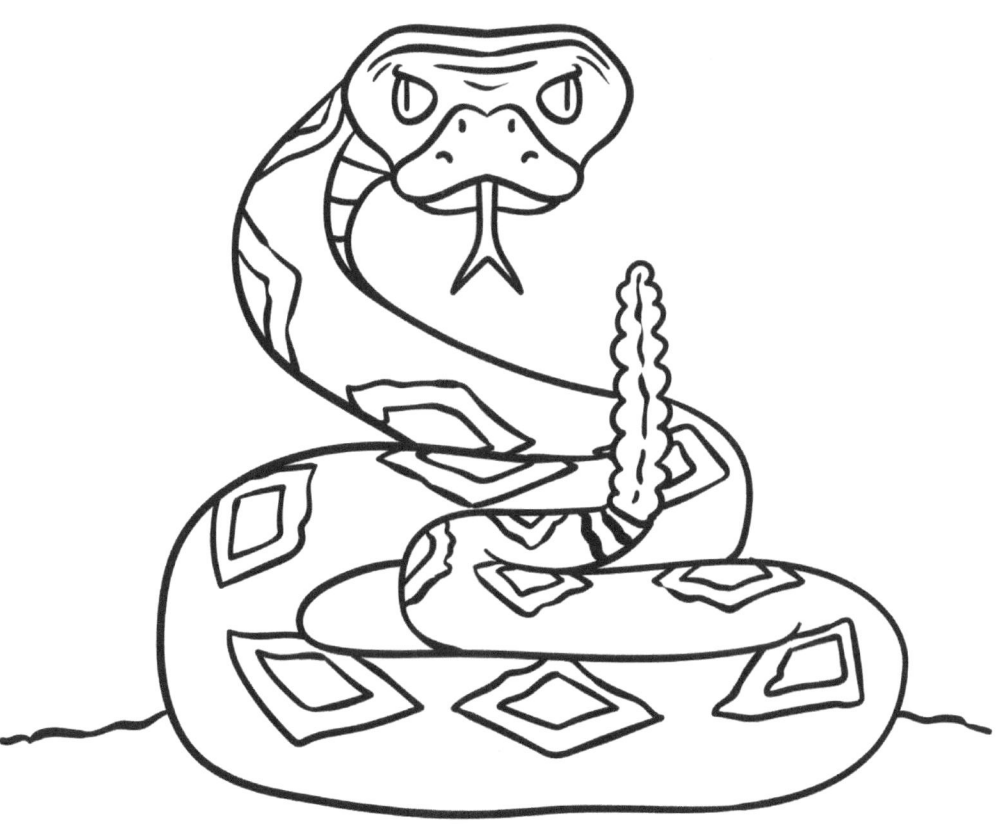

Snake

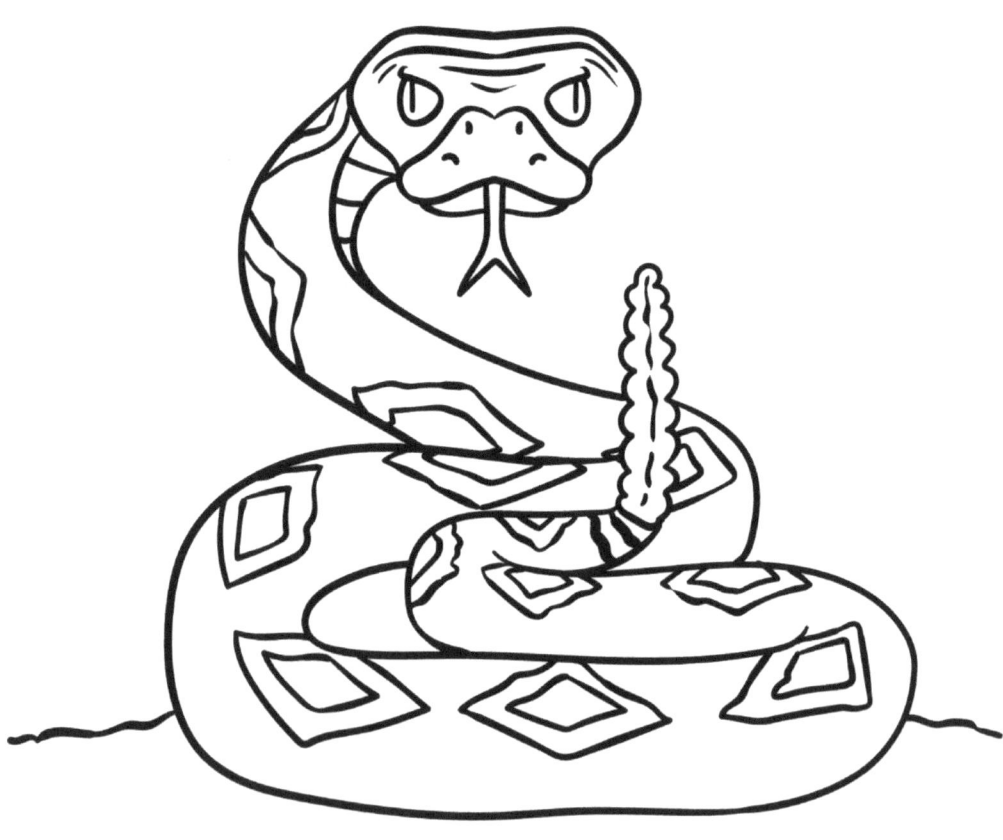

Snake

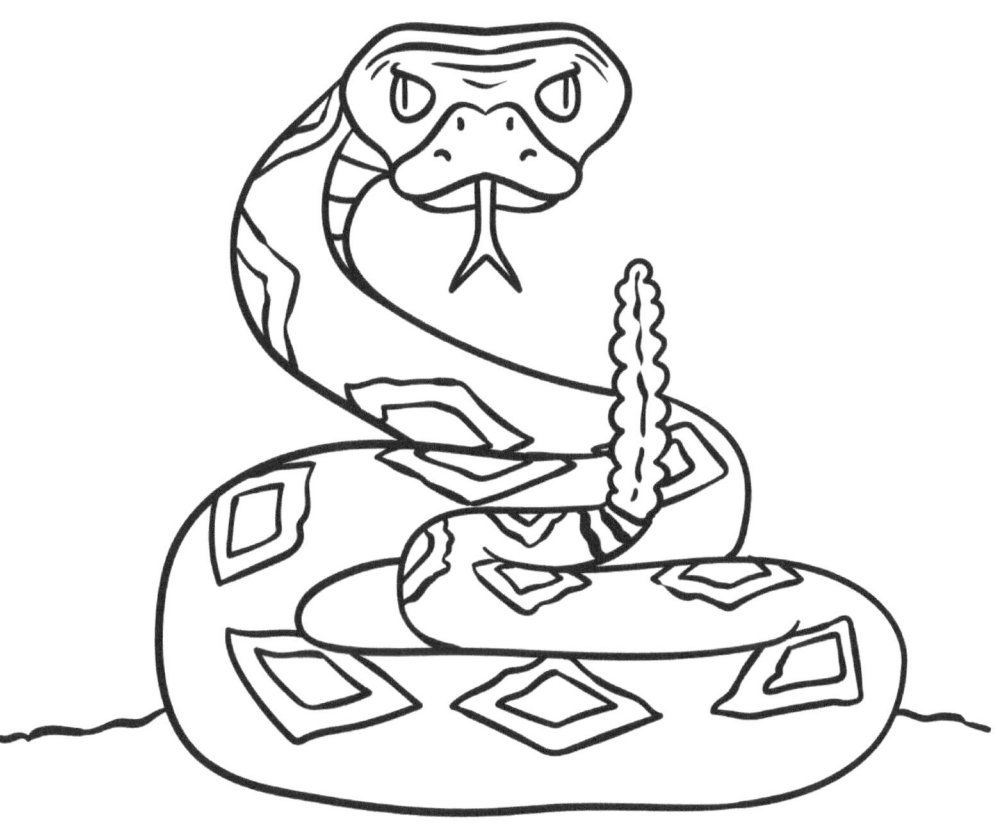

TABLE SUMMARIZING STEPS TO FOLLOW WHEN PAINTING A SKETCH OF A DOG:

Step	Description
1	Gather your materials: sketching paper, pencils, eraser, paints, and brushes.
2	Choose a reference image of a dog.
3	Start with a rough sketch, outlining the basic shape of the dog's body and head.
4	Add details such as the dog's eyes, nose, and ears.
5	Refine the sketch, erasing unnecessary lines and making adjustments.
6	Choose your painting technique (e.g., watercolours, acrylics).
7	Begin painting, starting with the background or larger areas of colour.
8	Add depth and shadows with darker shades or mix in black or brown.
9	Fine-tune the details, adding fur texture and highlighting the dog's features.
10	Make any final adjustments or touch-ups. Sign your artwork if desired.

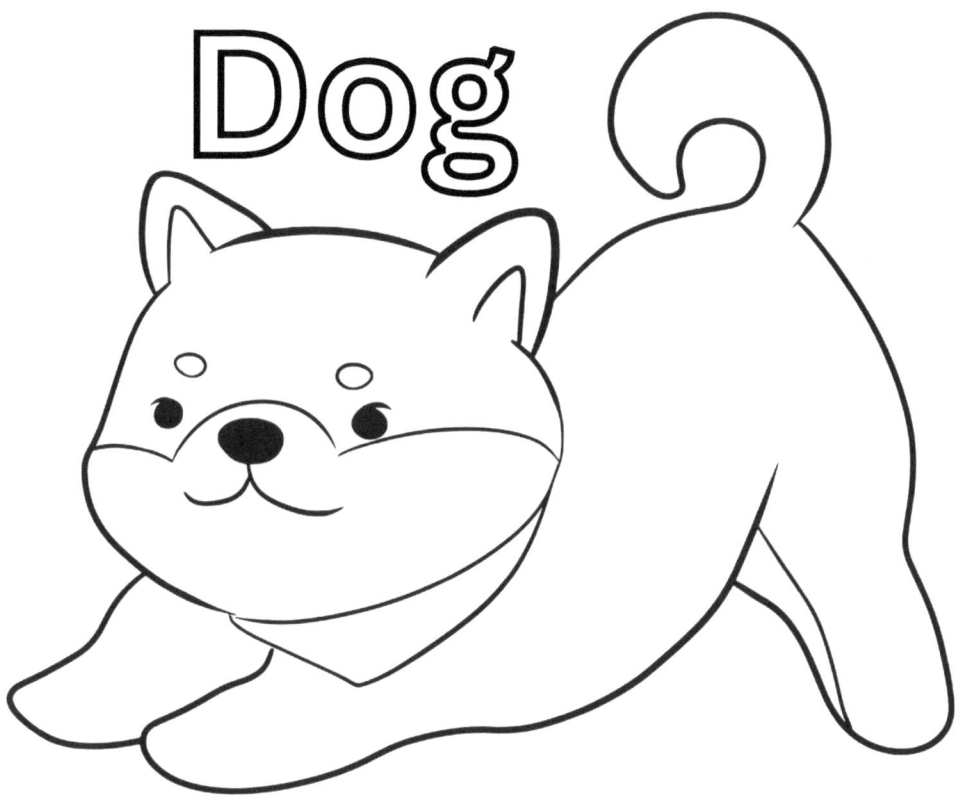

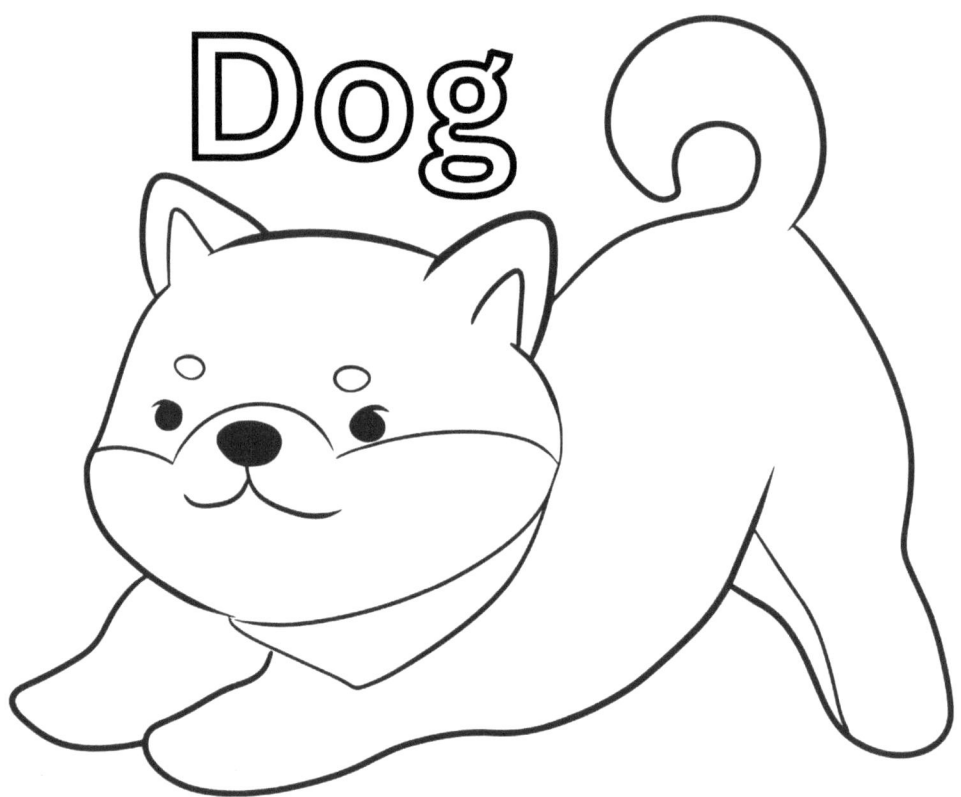

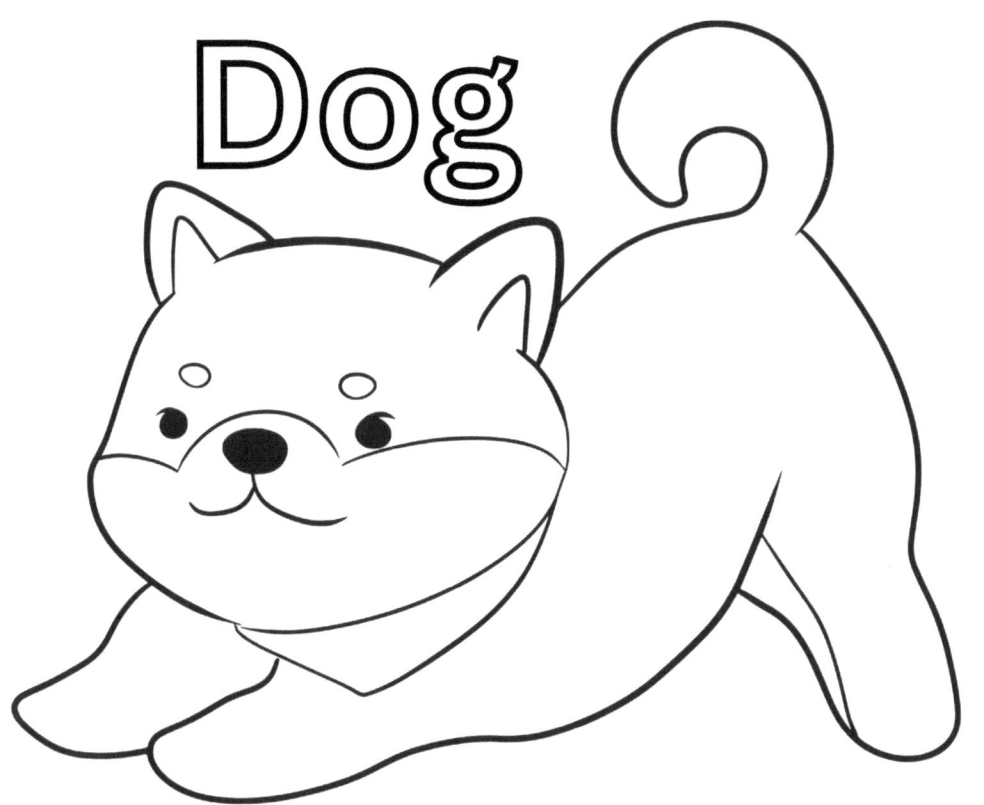

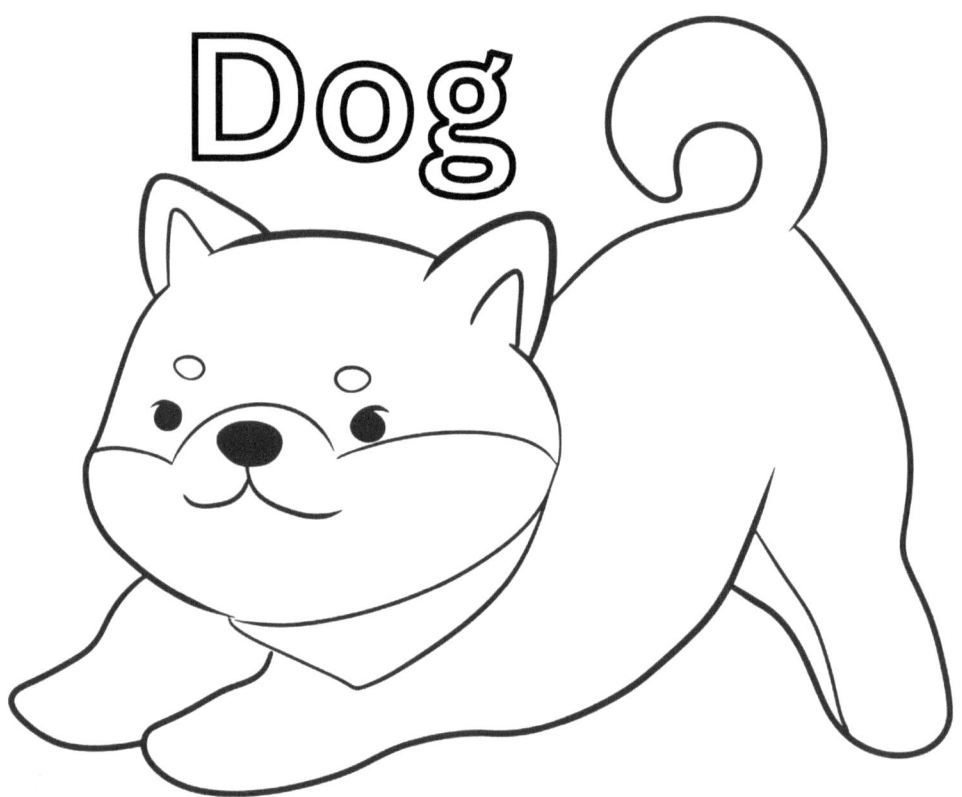

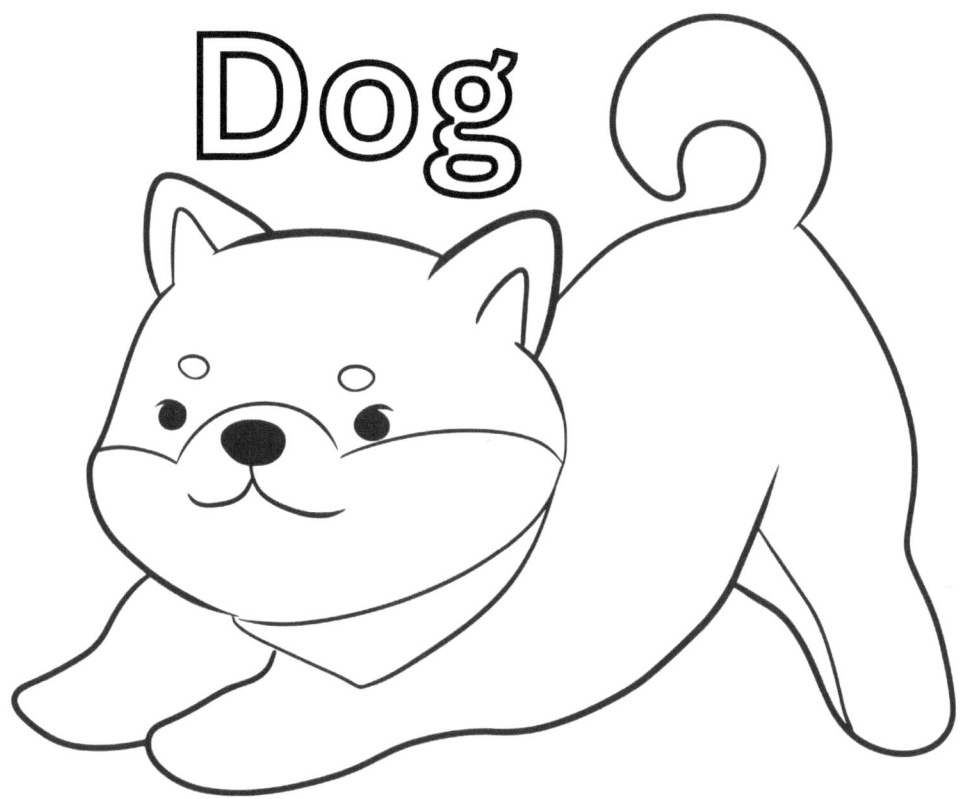

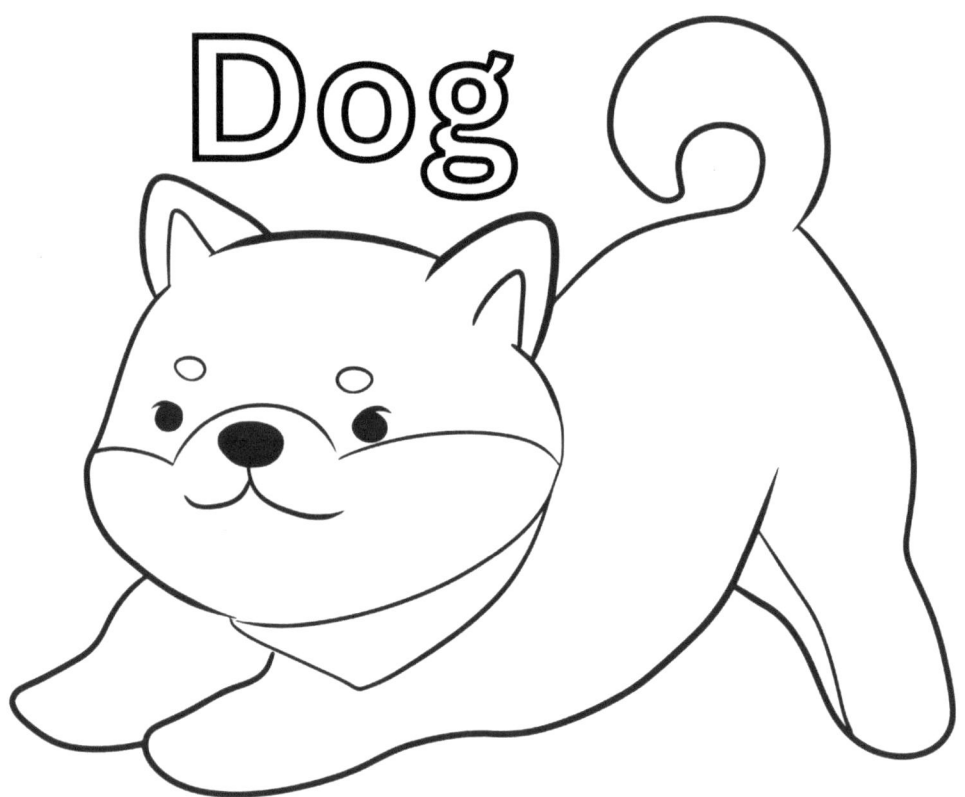

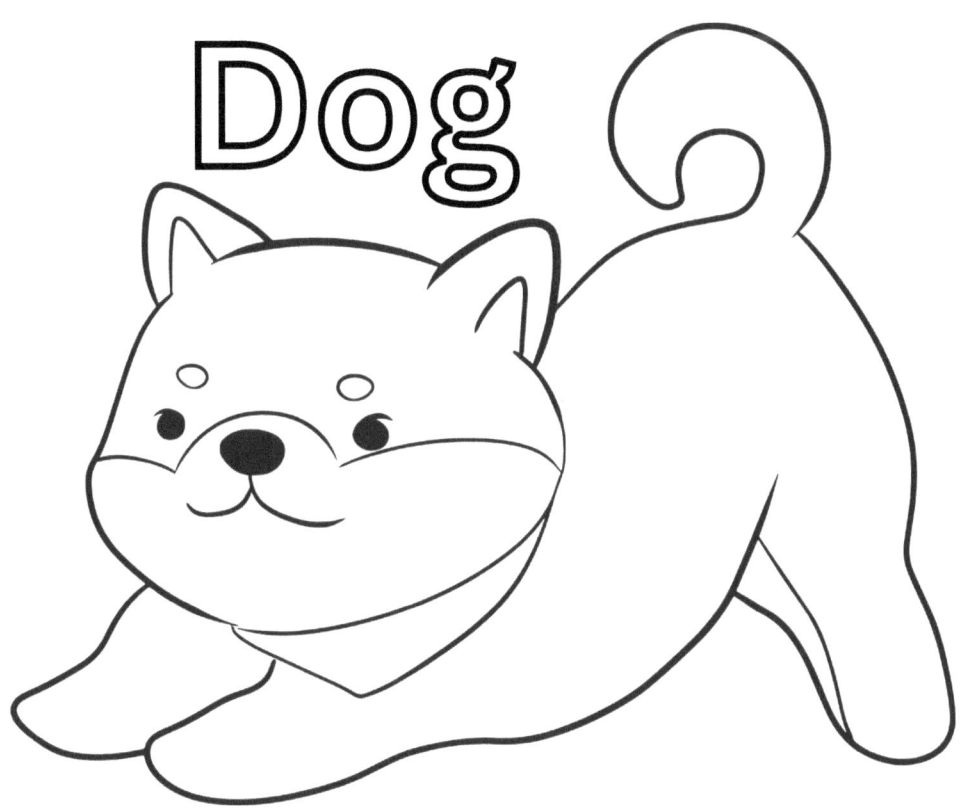

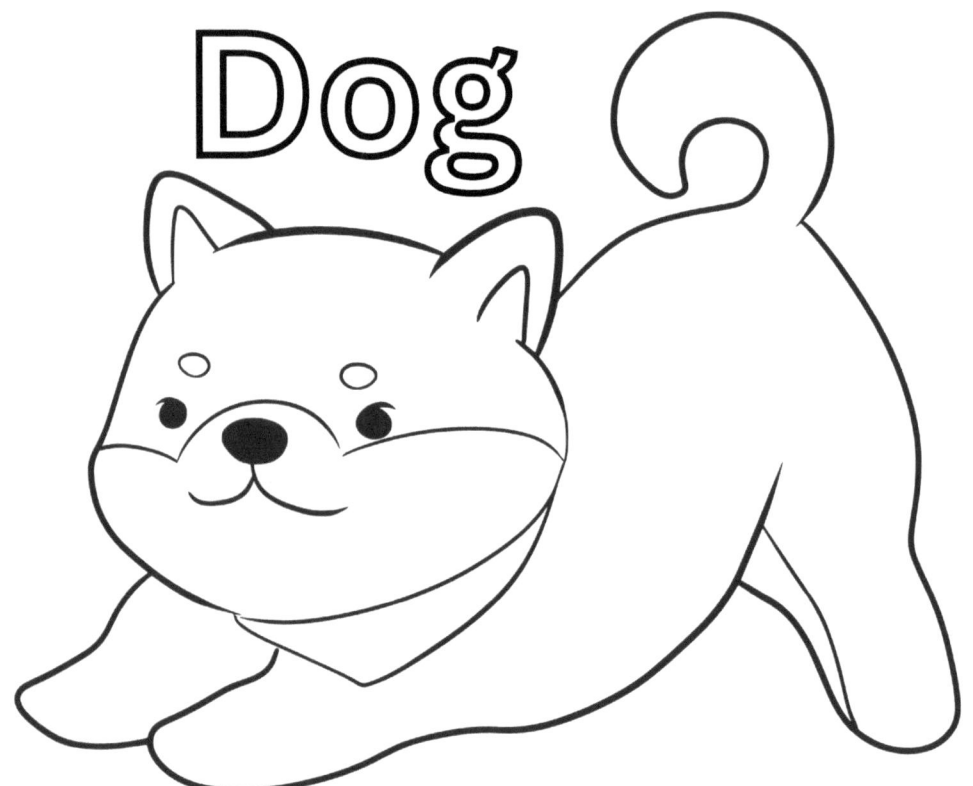

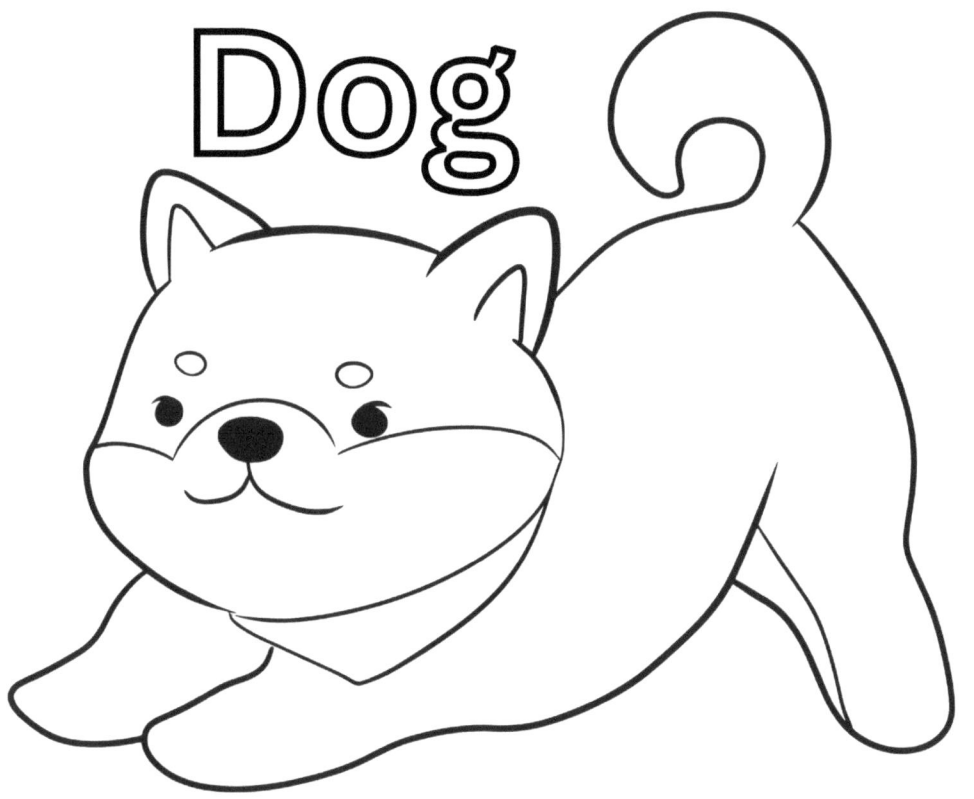

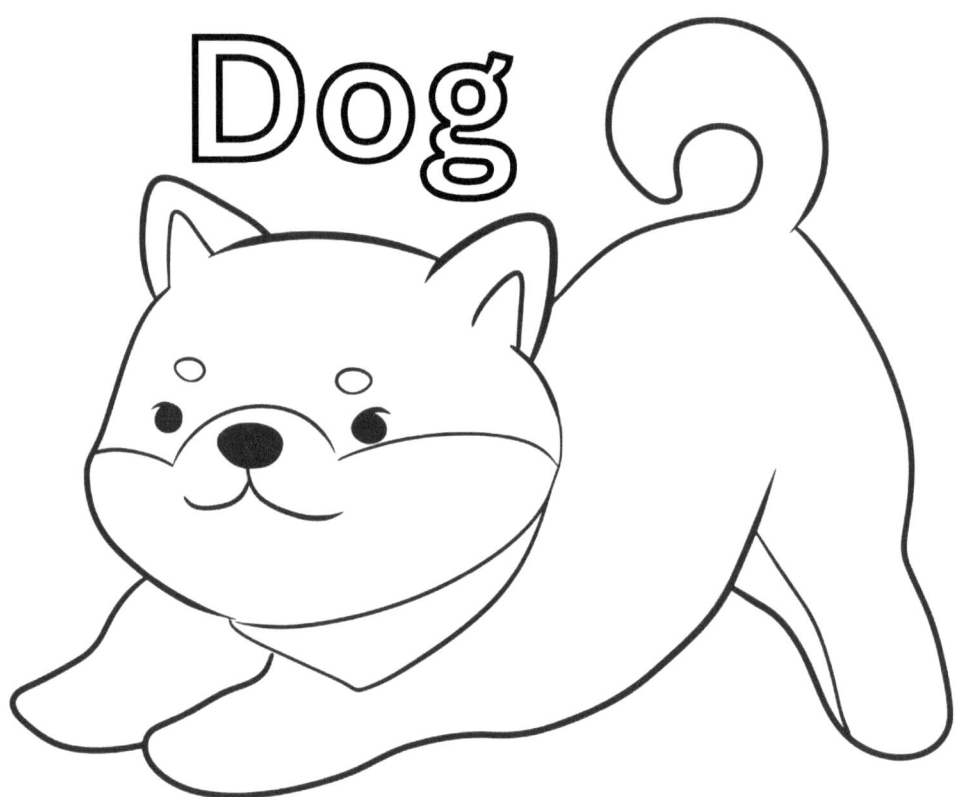

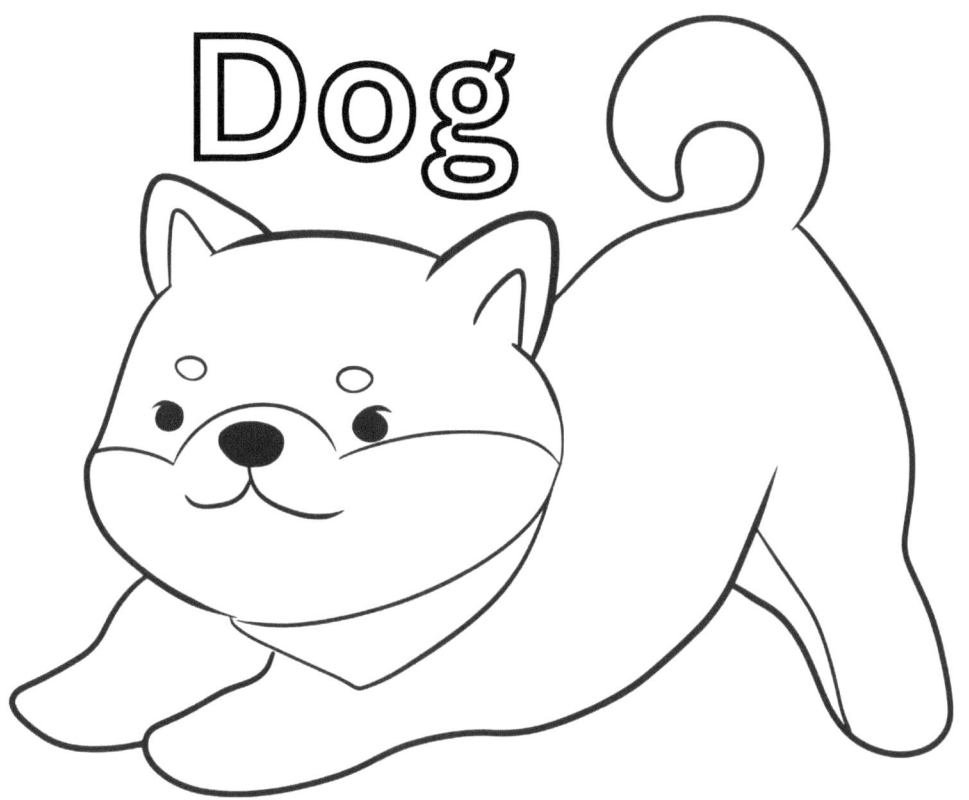

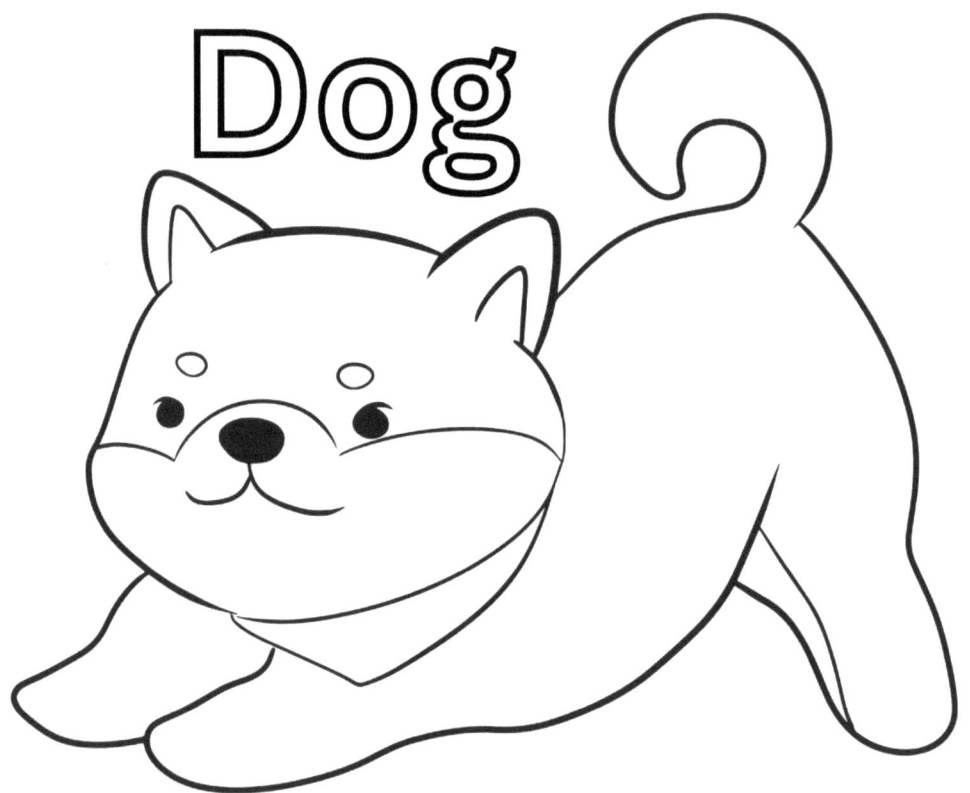

TABLE SUMMARIZING
STEPS TO FOLLOW WHEN PAINTING A SKETCH OF A FISH:

Step	Description
1	Gather your materials: sketching paper, pencils, eraser, paints, and brushes.
2	Choose a reference image of a fish.
3	Start with a rough sketch, outlining the basic shape of the fish's body.
4	Add details such as the fish's fins, tail, and mouth.
5	Refine the sketch, erasing unnecessary lines and making adjustments.
6	Choose your painting technique (e.g., watercolours, acrylics).
7	Begin painting, starting with the background or larger areas of colour.
8	Add depth and shadows with darker shades or mix in black or brown.
9	Fine-tune the details, adding scales and patterns to the fish's body.
10	Make any final adjustments or touch-ups. Sign your artwork if desired.

Fish

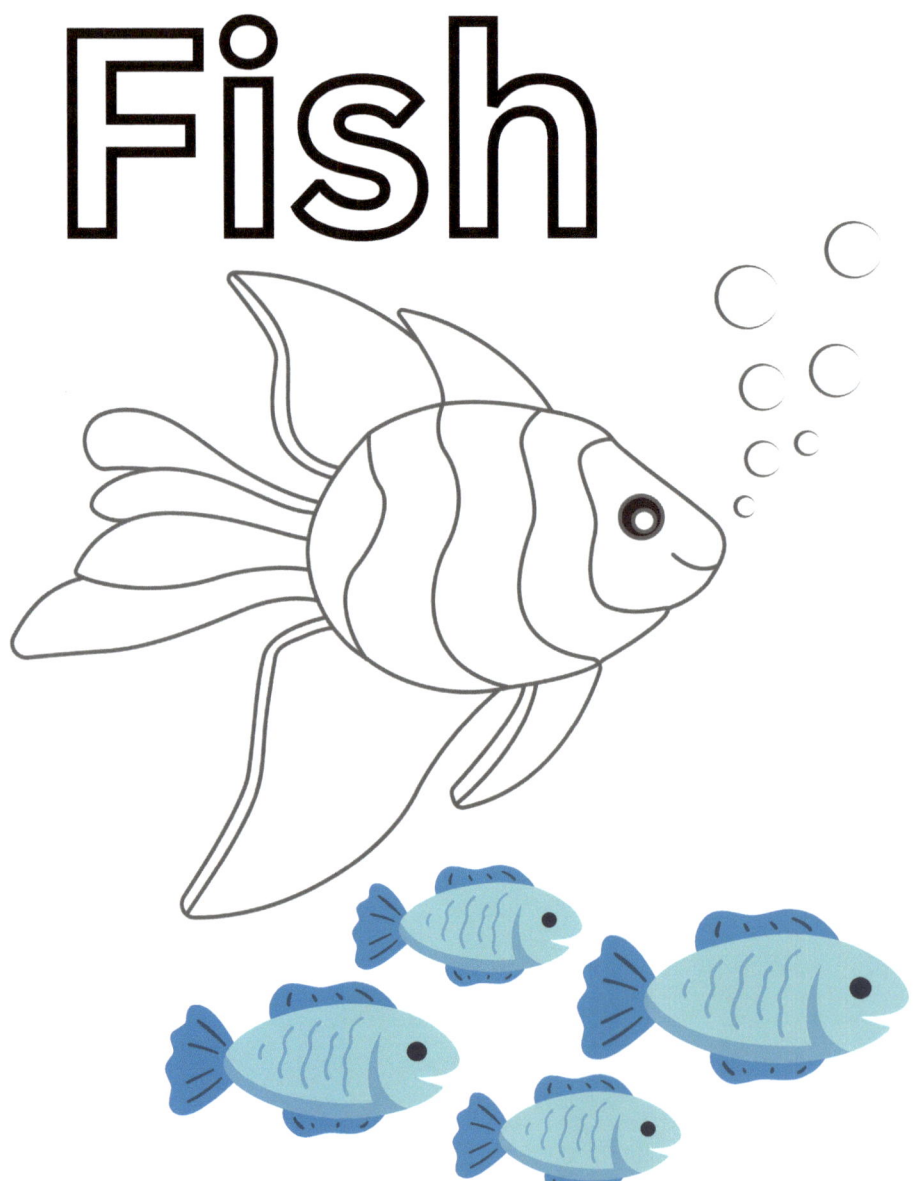

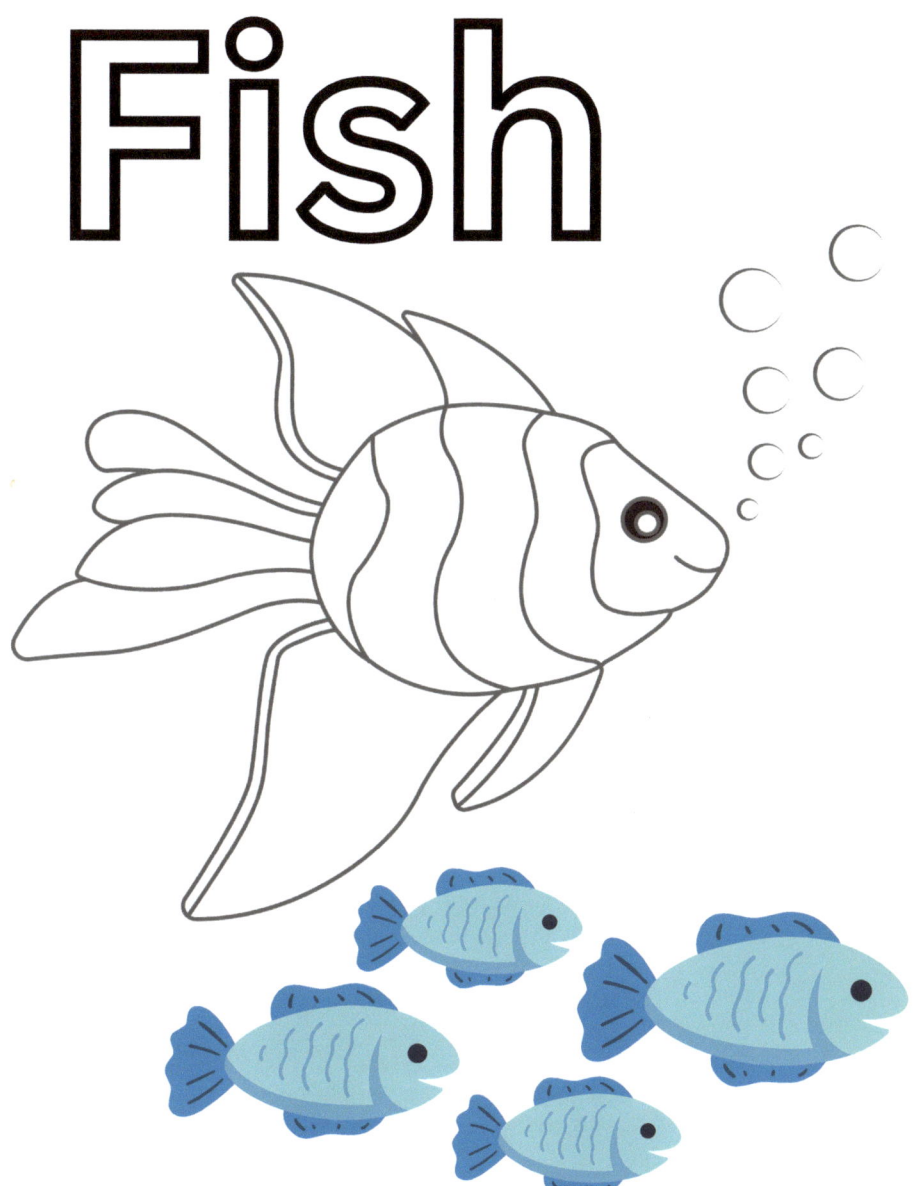

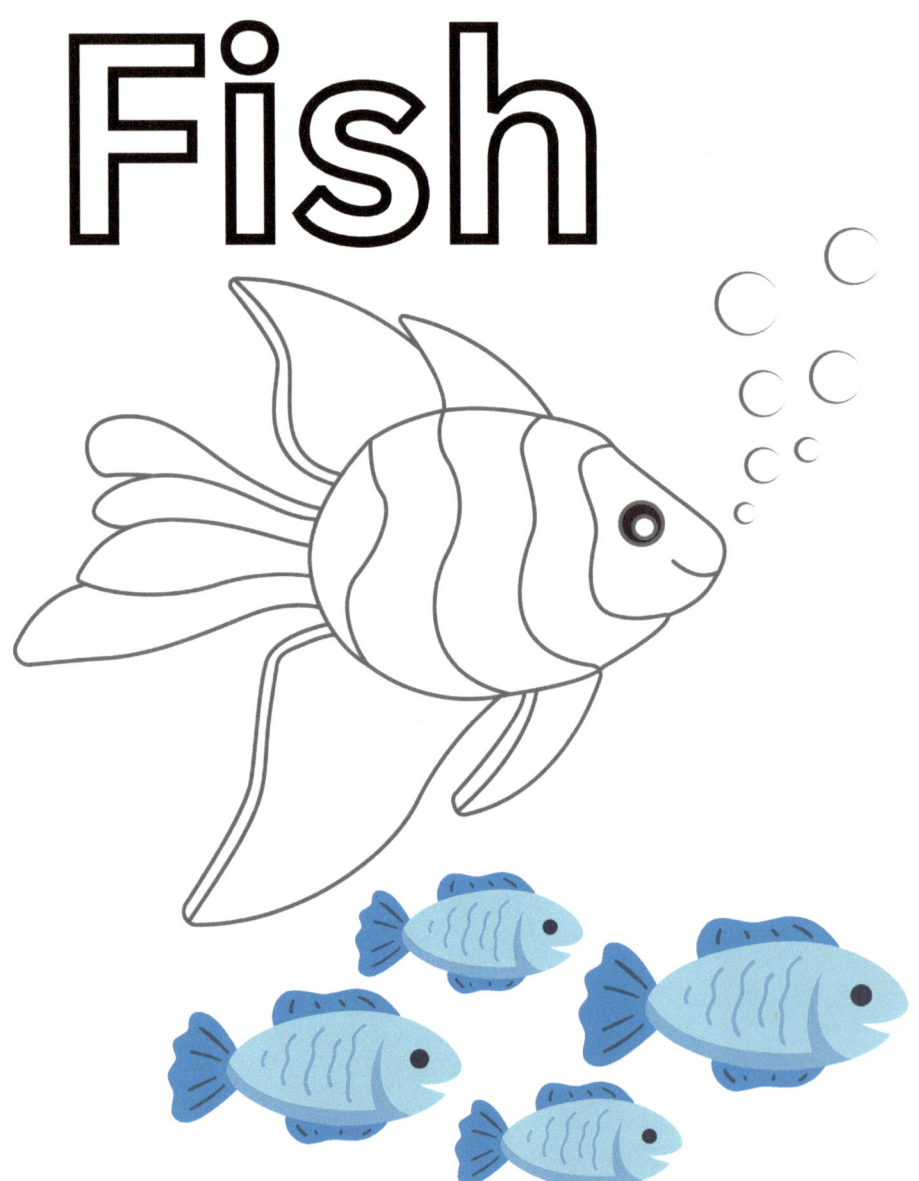

Fish

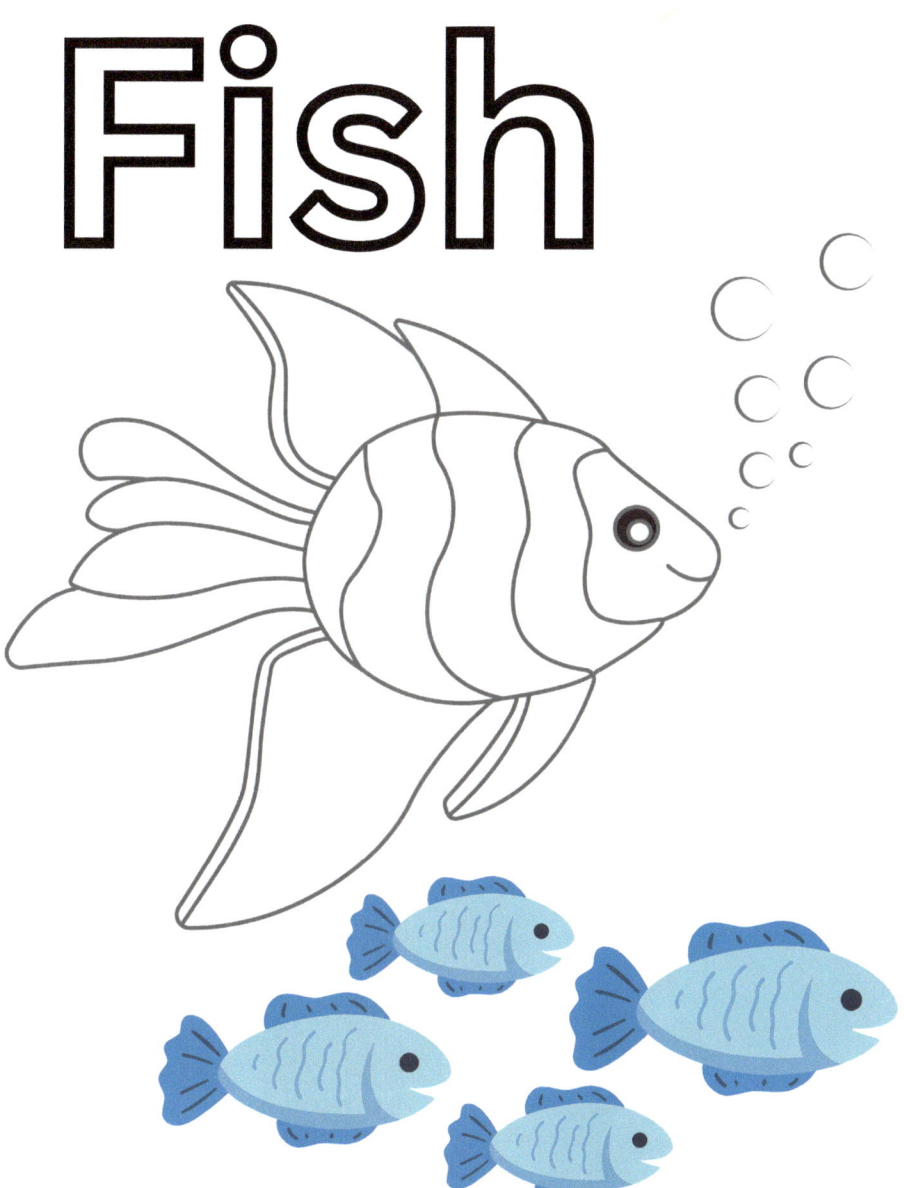

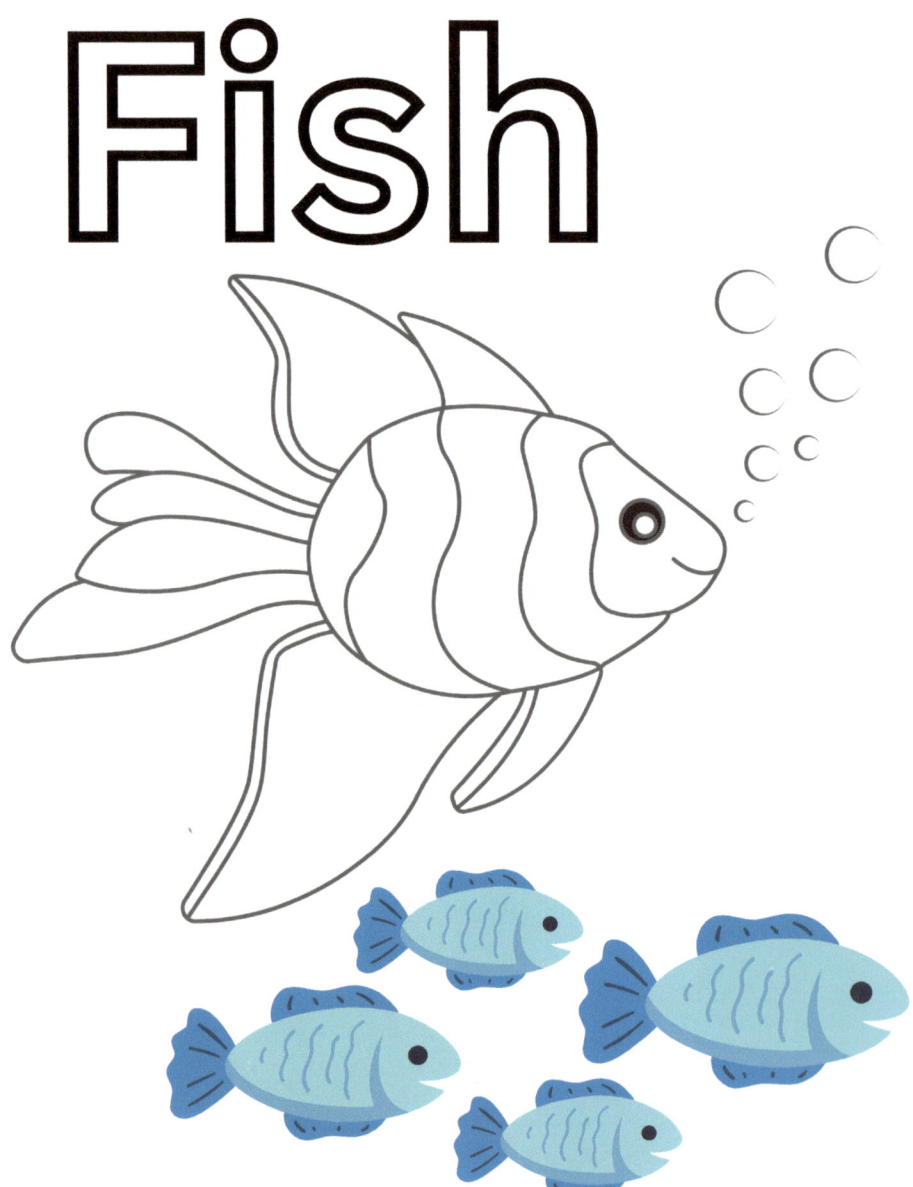

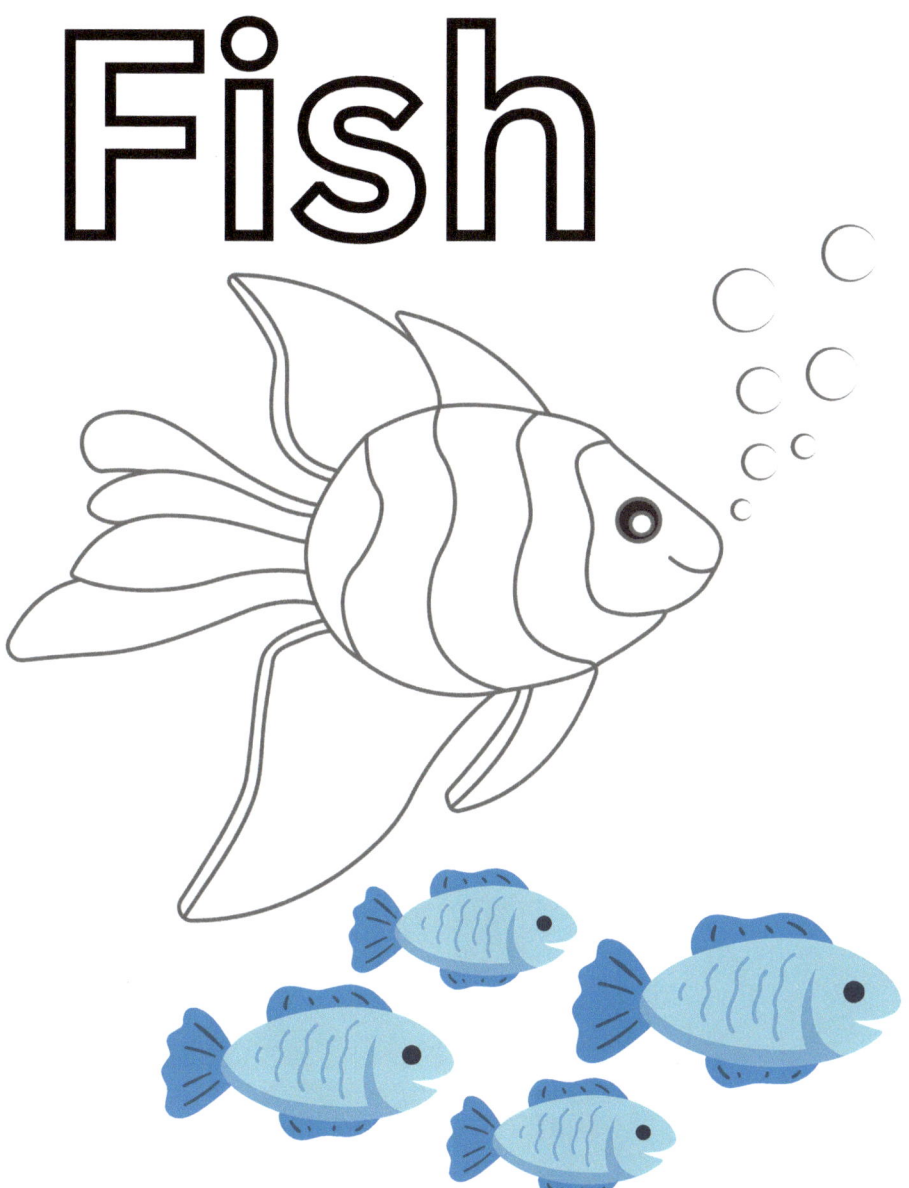

Fish

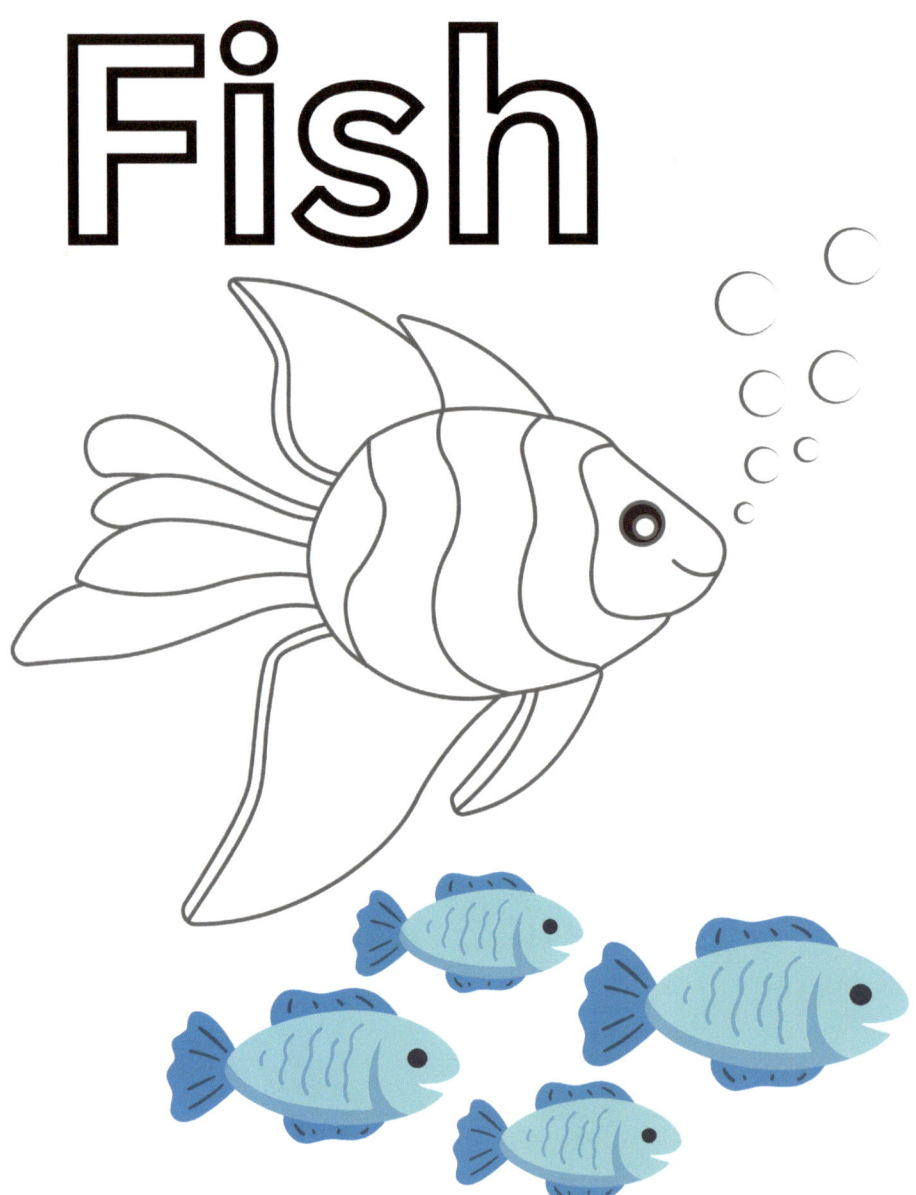

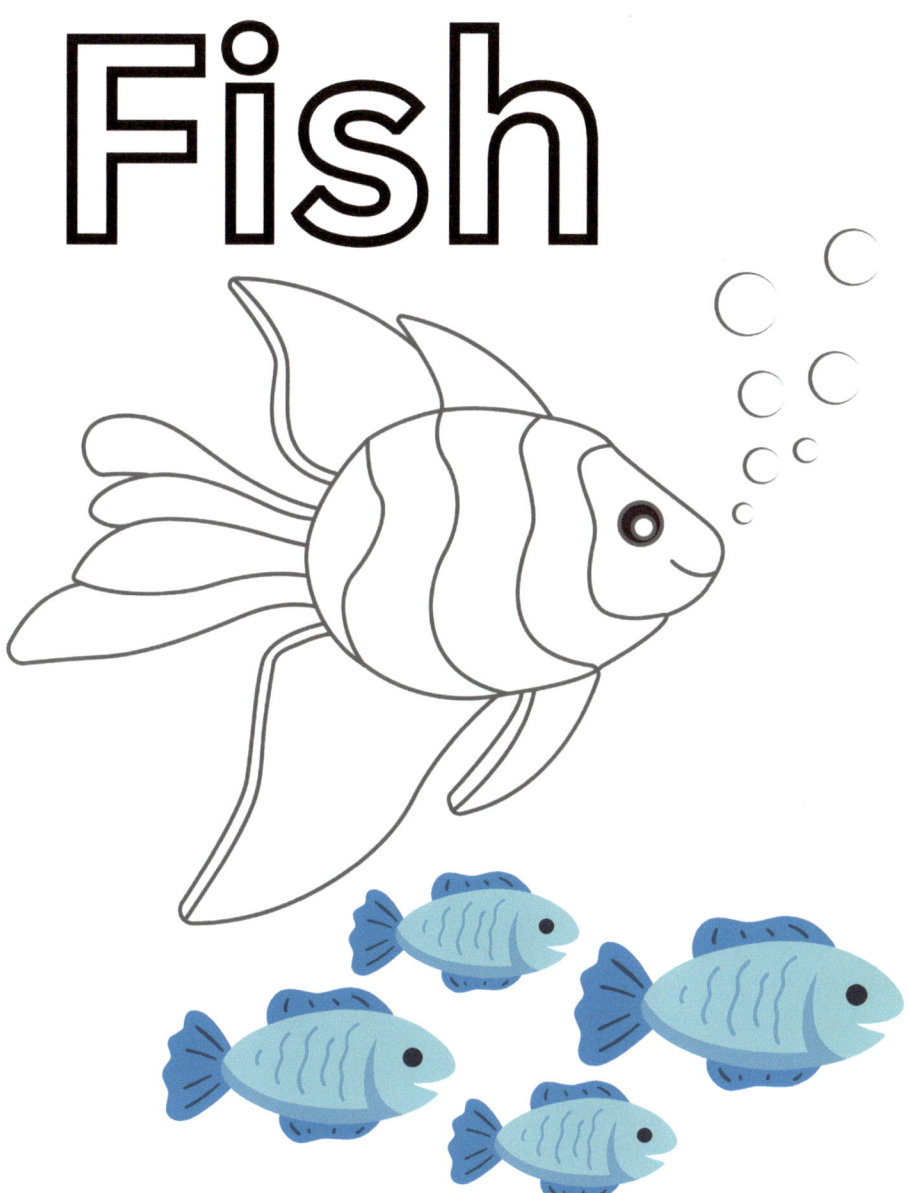

Fish

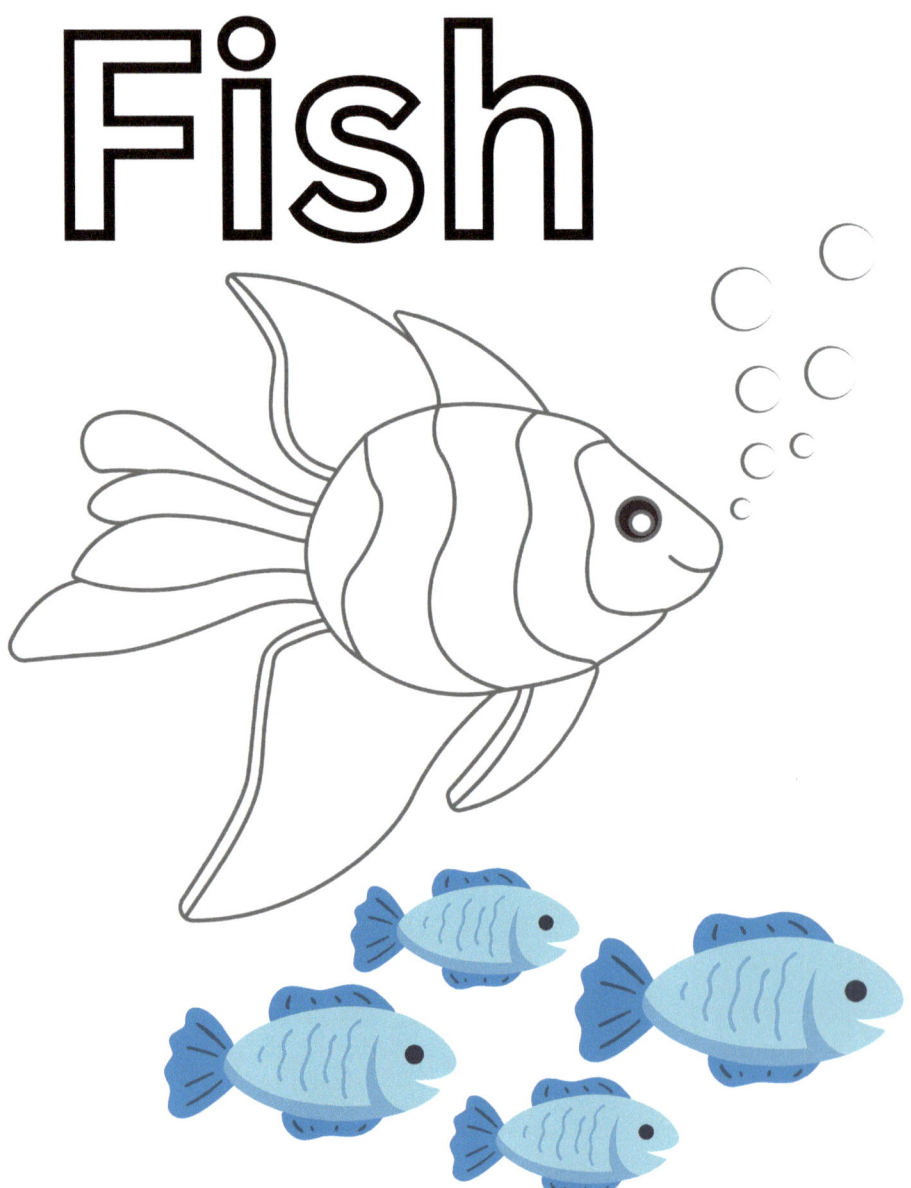

Fish

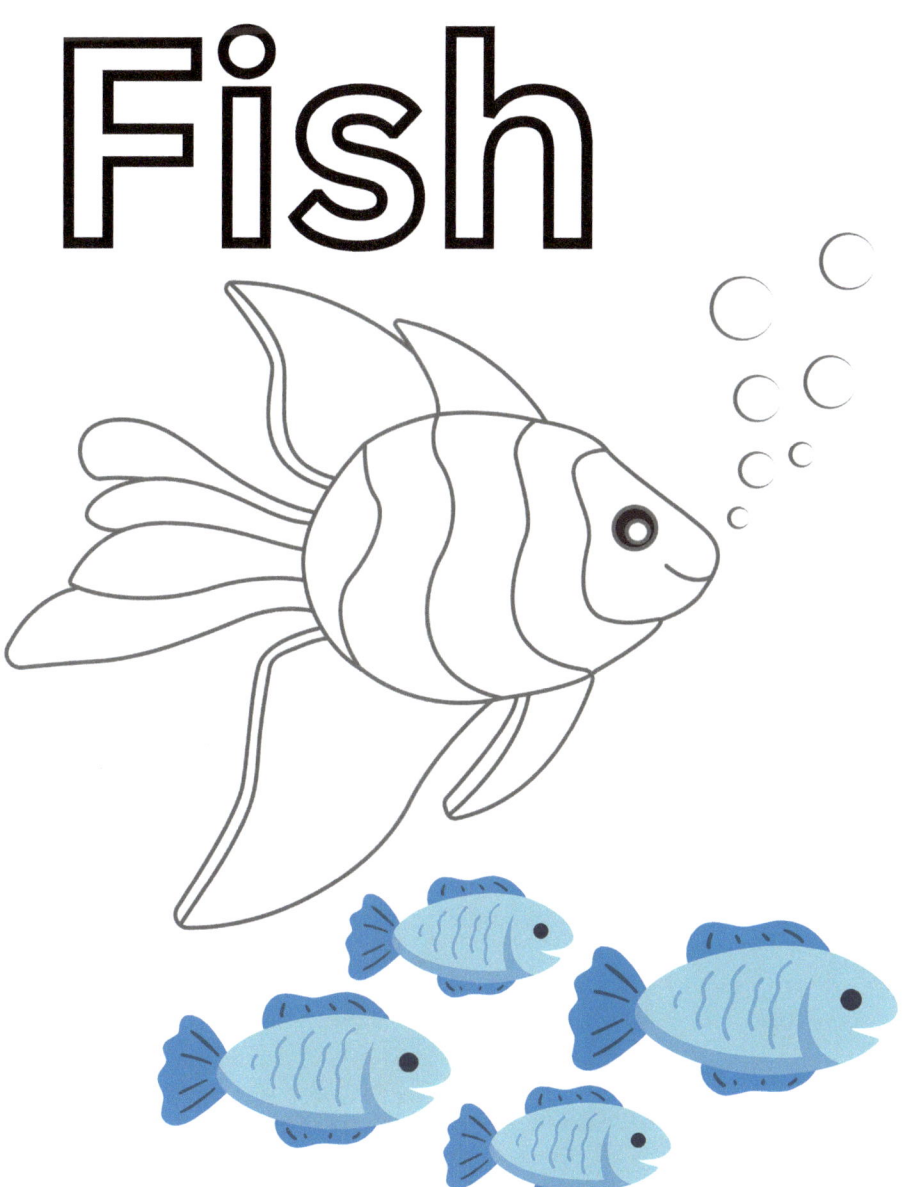

TABLE SUMMARIZING
STEPS TO FOLLOW WHEN PAINTING A SKETCH OF A BEAR:

Step	Description
1	Gather your materials: sketching paper, pencils, eraser, paints, and brushes.
2	Choose a reference image of a bear.
3	Start with a rough sketch, outlining the basic shape of the bear's body.
4	Add details such as the bear's head, ears, and facial features.
5	Refine the sketch, erasing unnecessary lines and making adjustments.
6	Choose your painting technique (e.g., watercolours, acrylics).
7	Begin painting, starting with the background or larger areas of colour.
8	Add depth and shadows with darker shades or mix in black or brown.
9	Fine-tune the details, adding fur texture and highlighting the bear's features.
10	Make any final adjustments or touch-ups. Sign your artwork if desired.

Bear

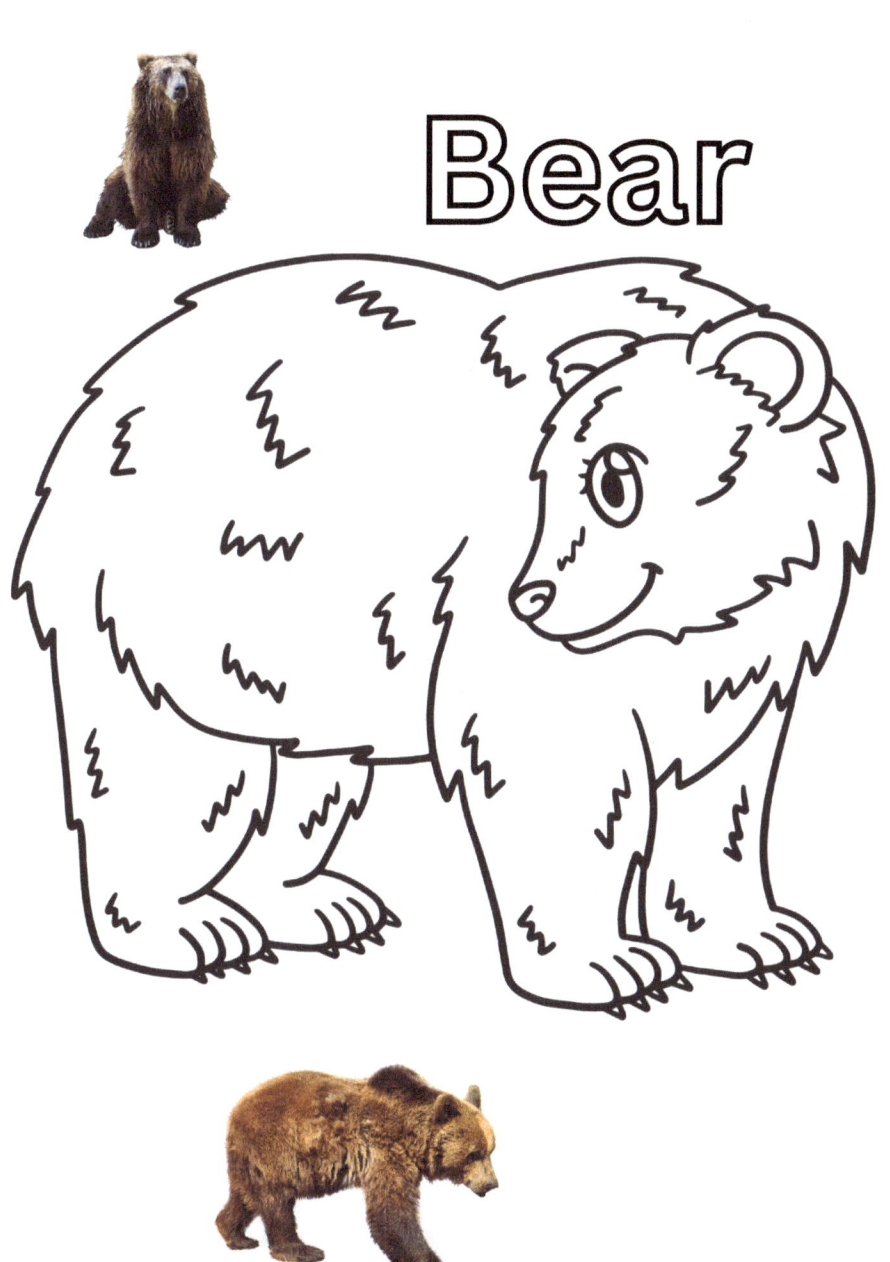

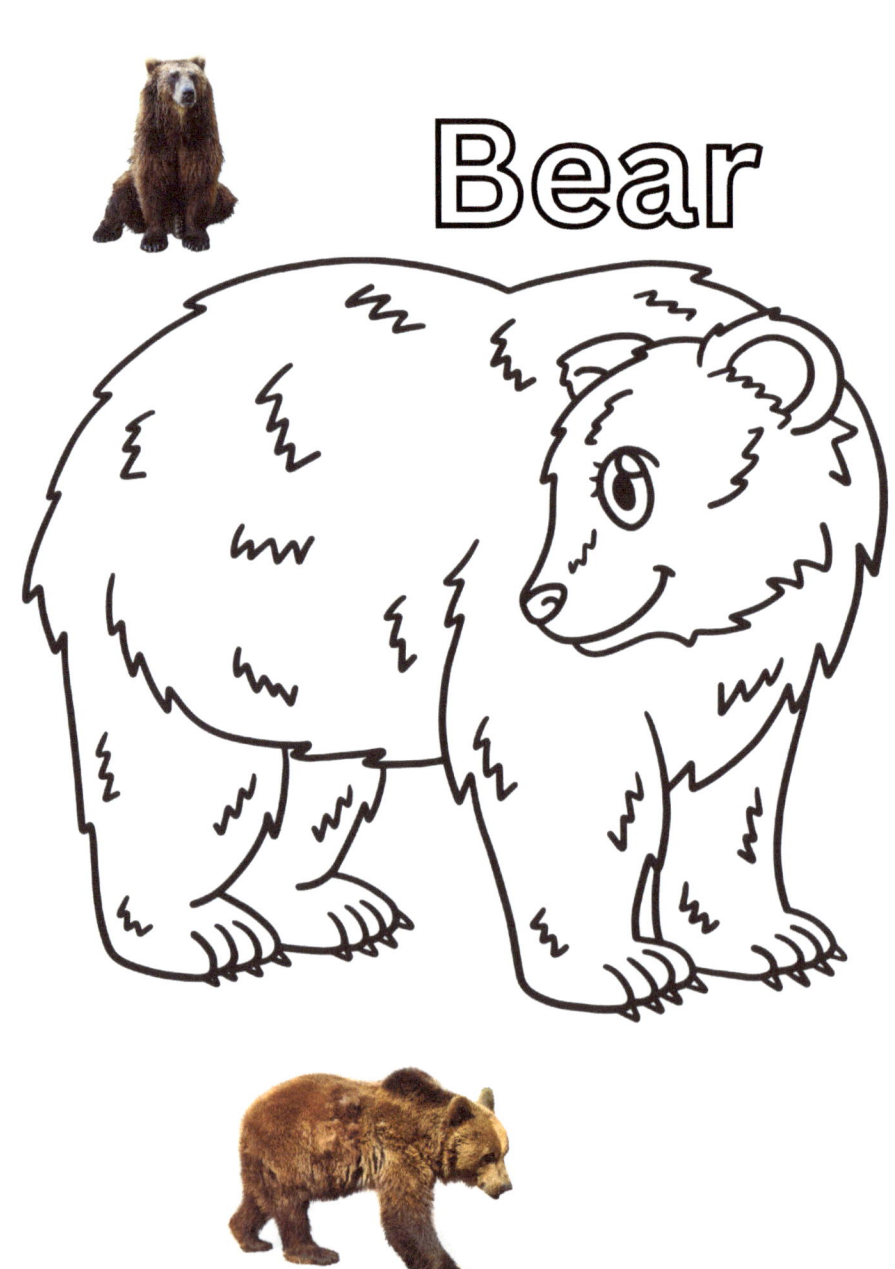

Bear

Bear

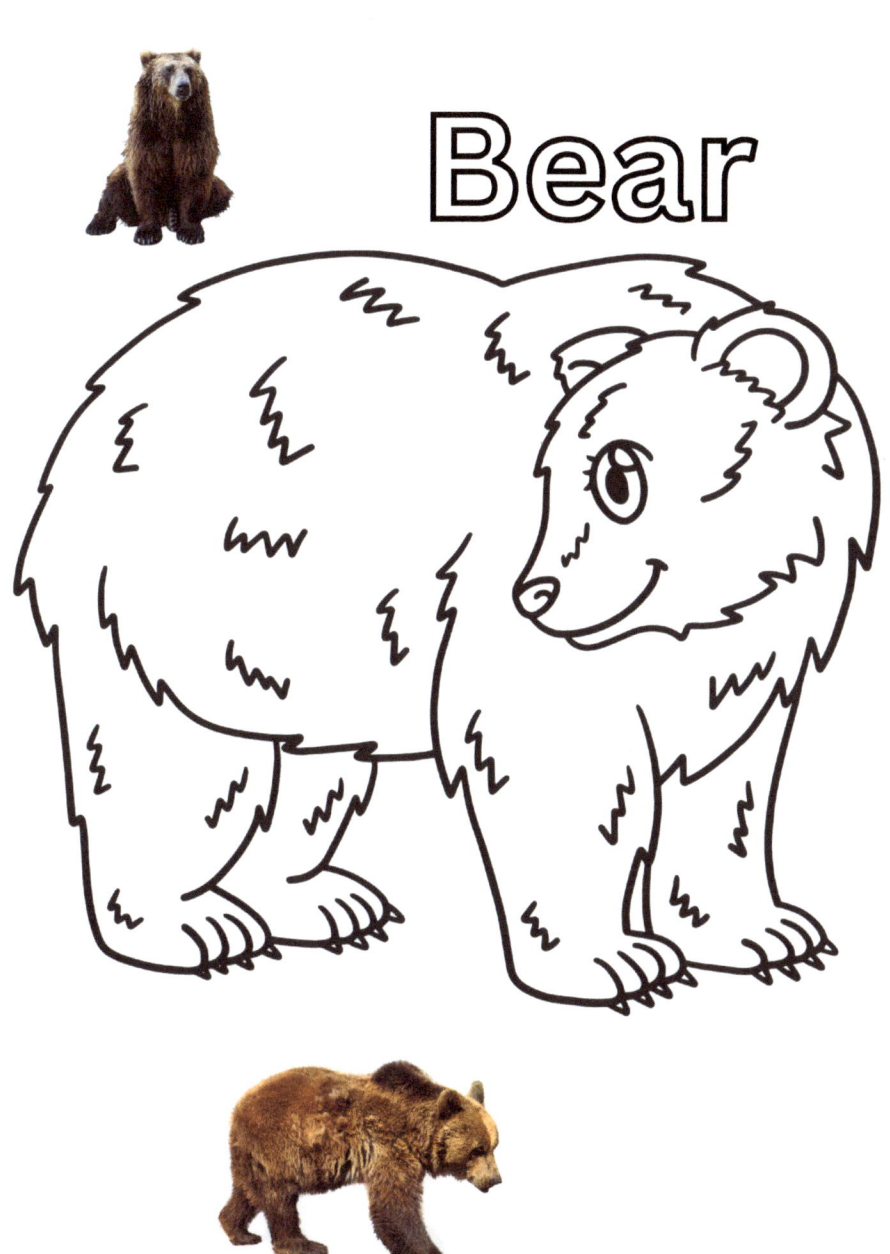

Bear

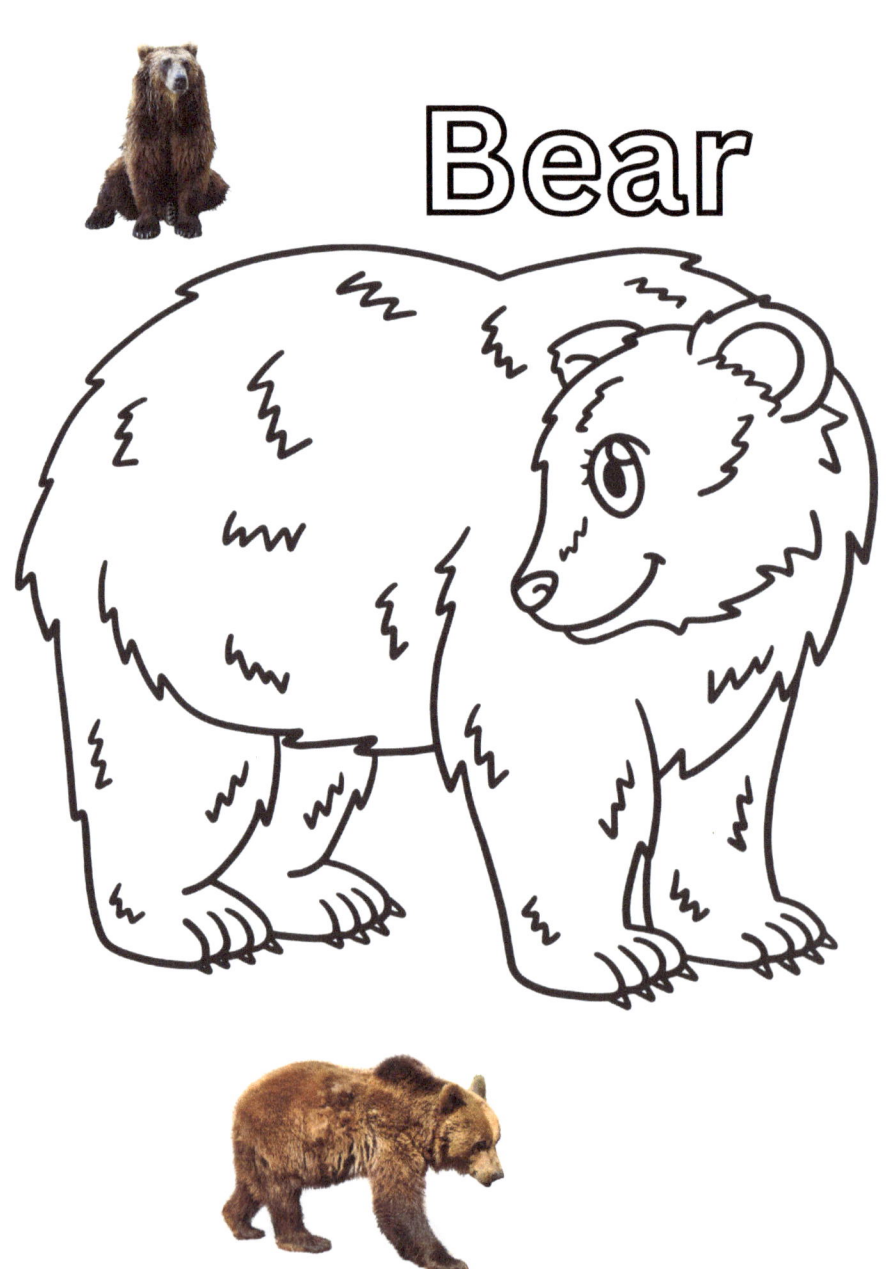

Bear

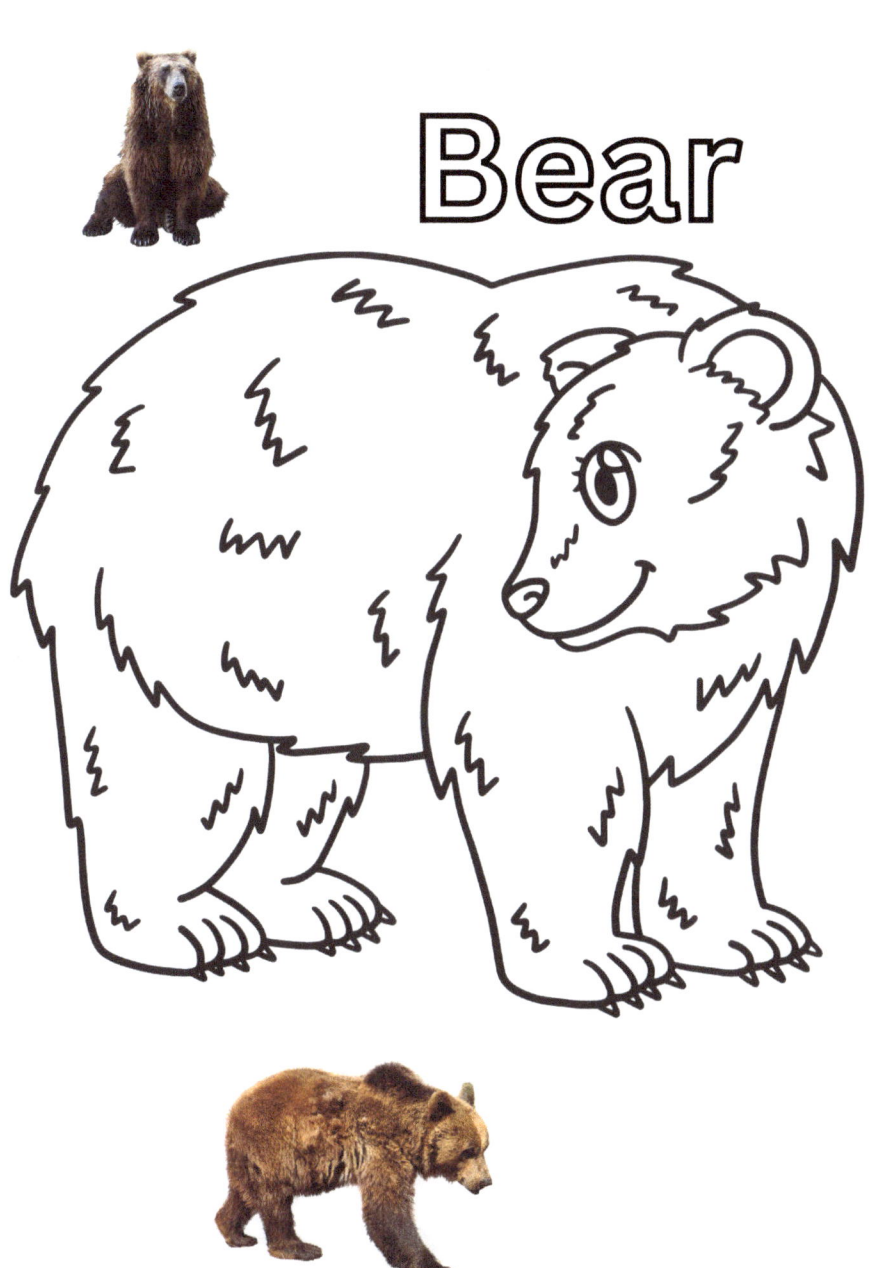

Bear

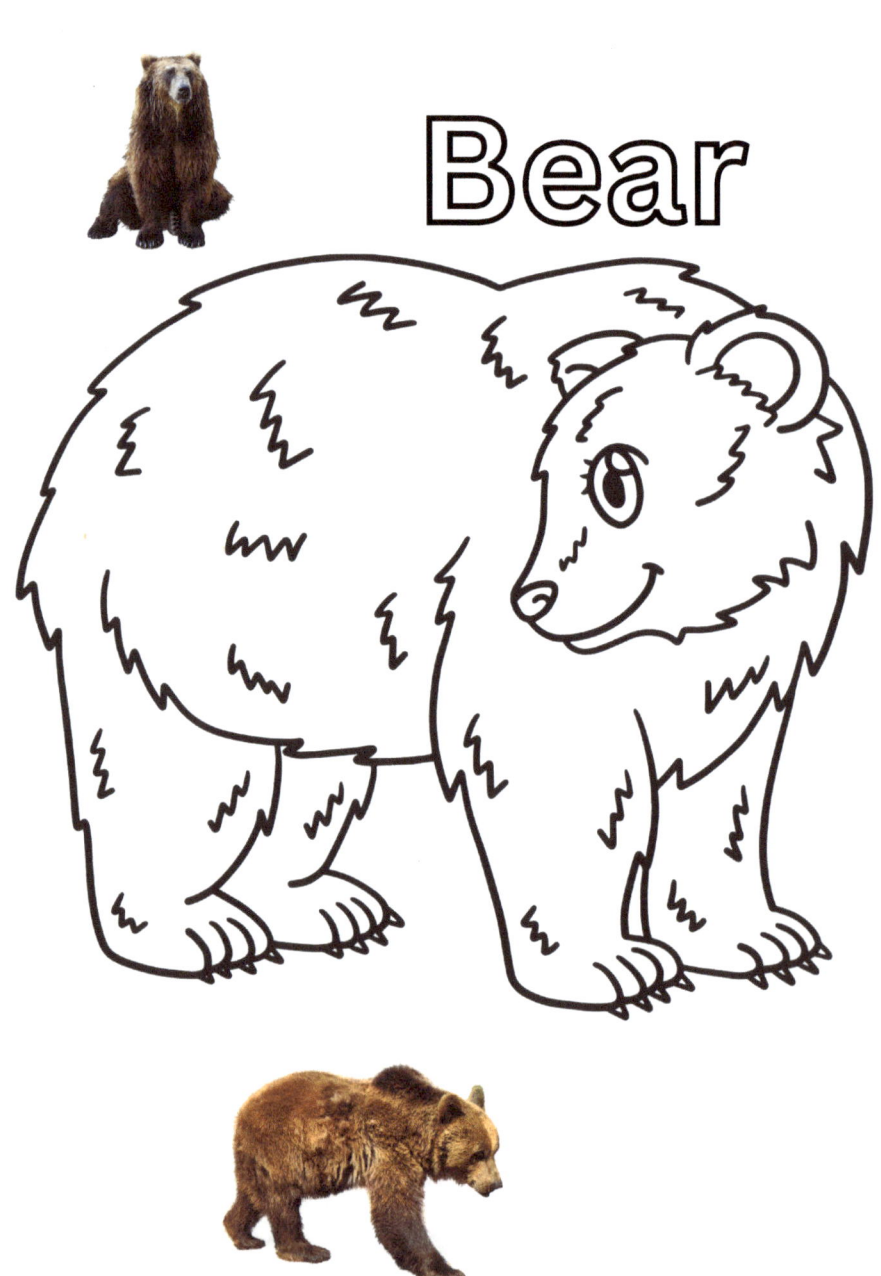

Bear

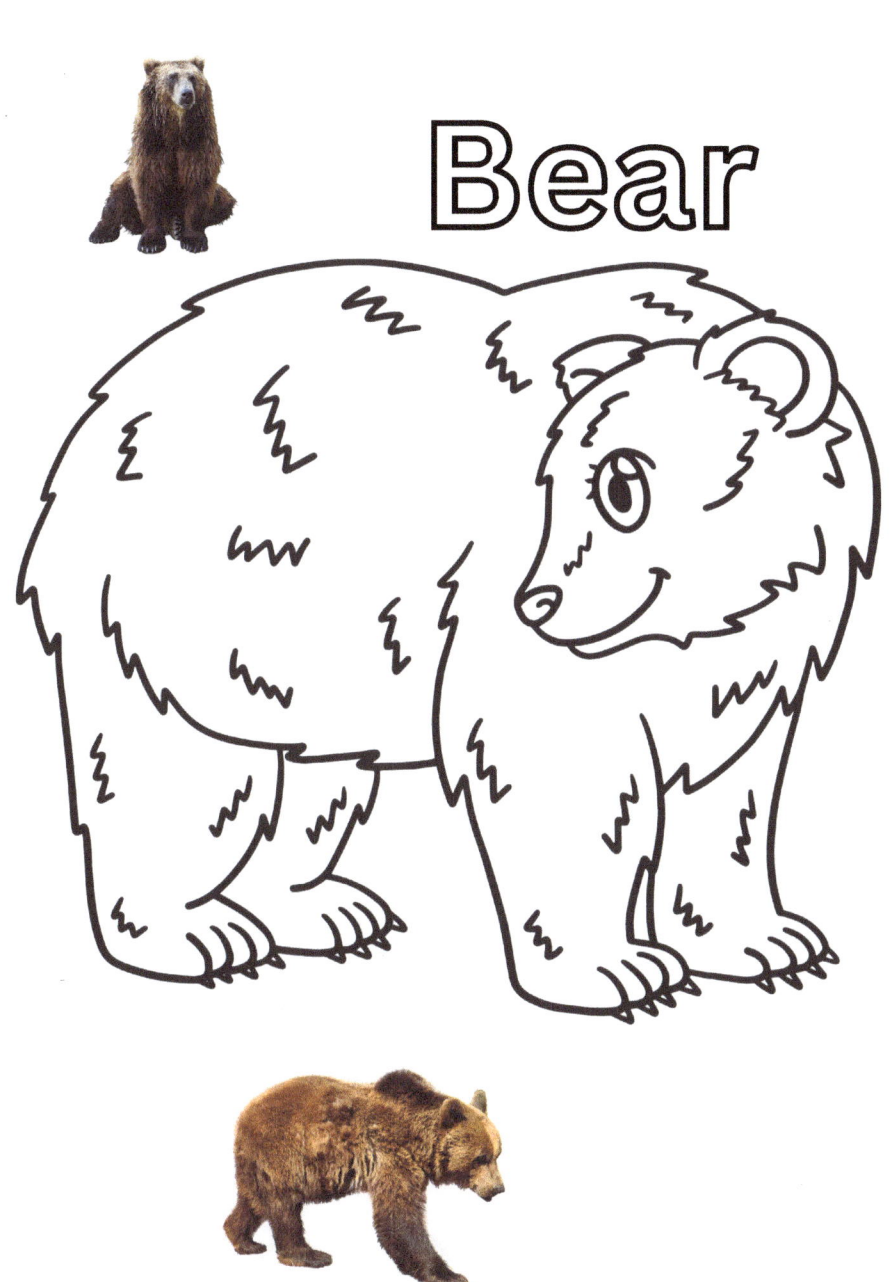

Bear

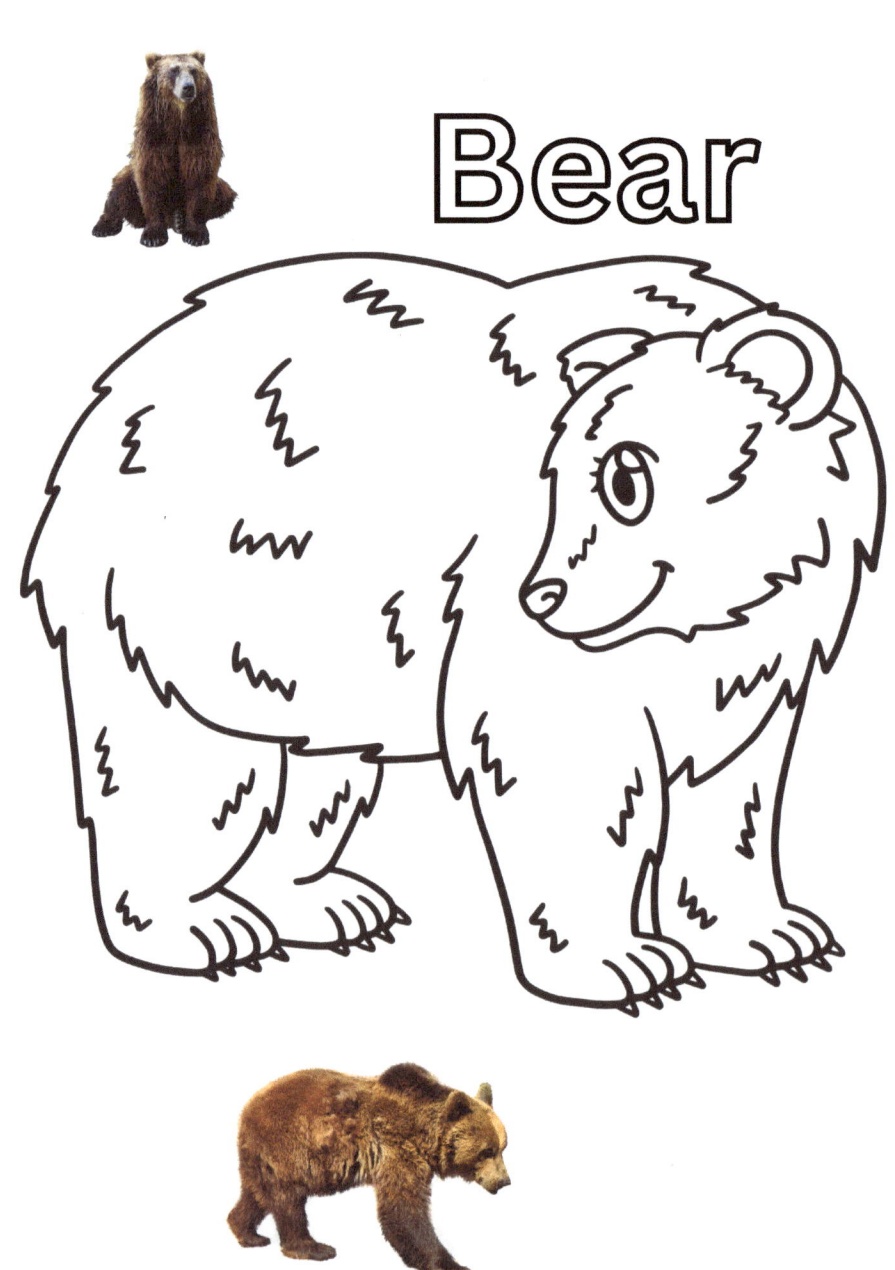

Bear

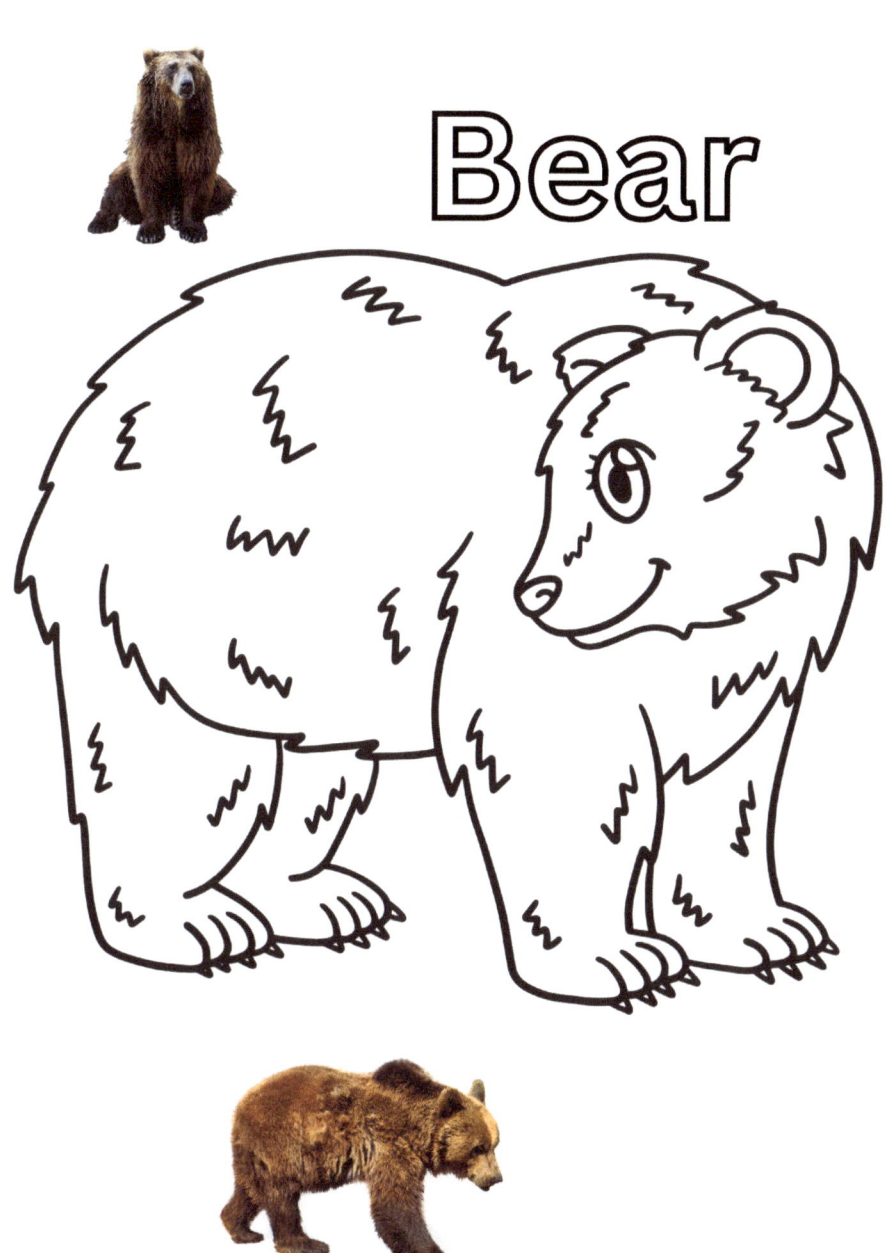

Bear

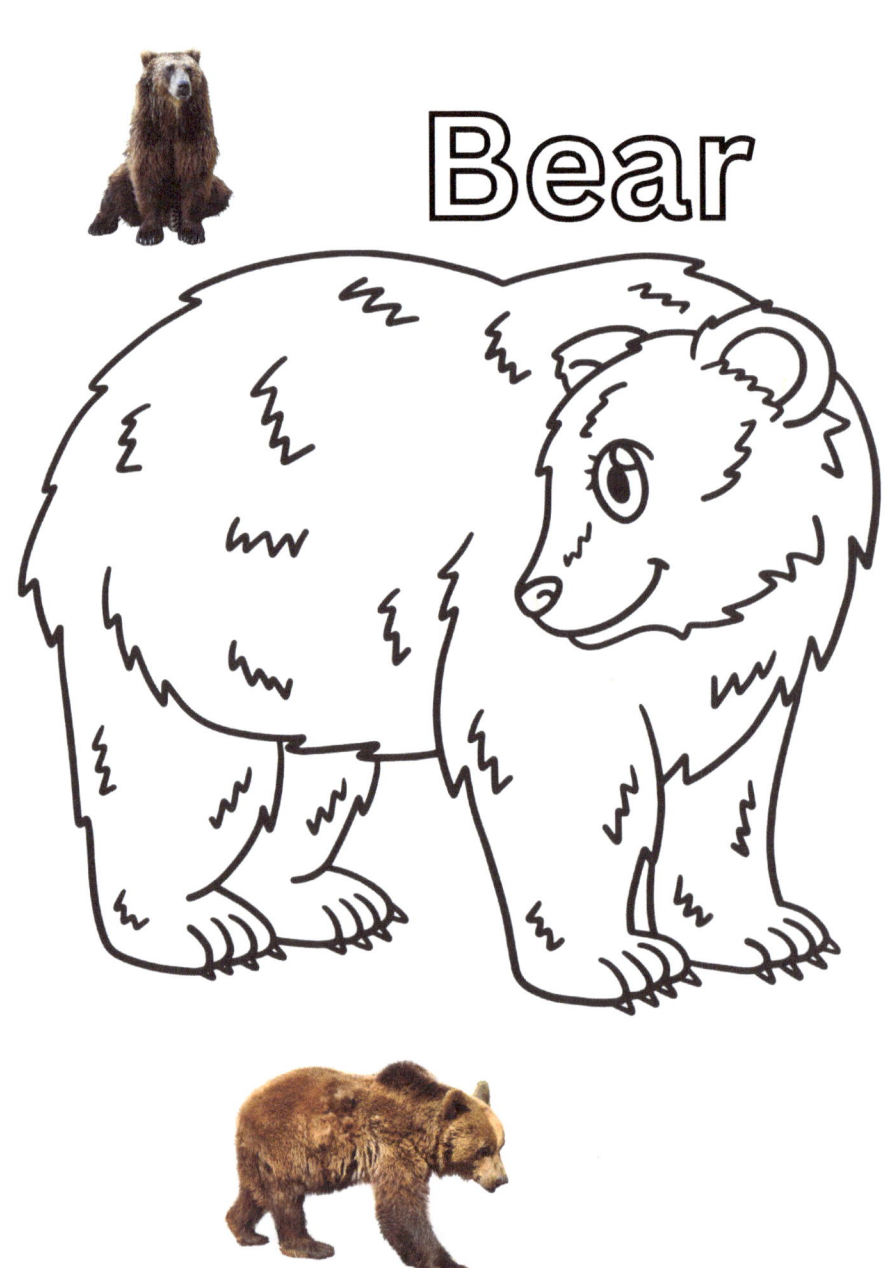

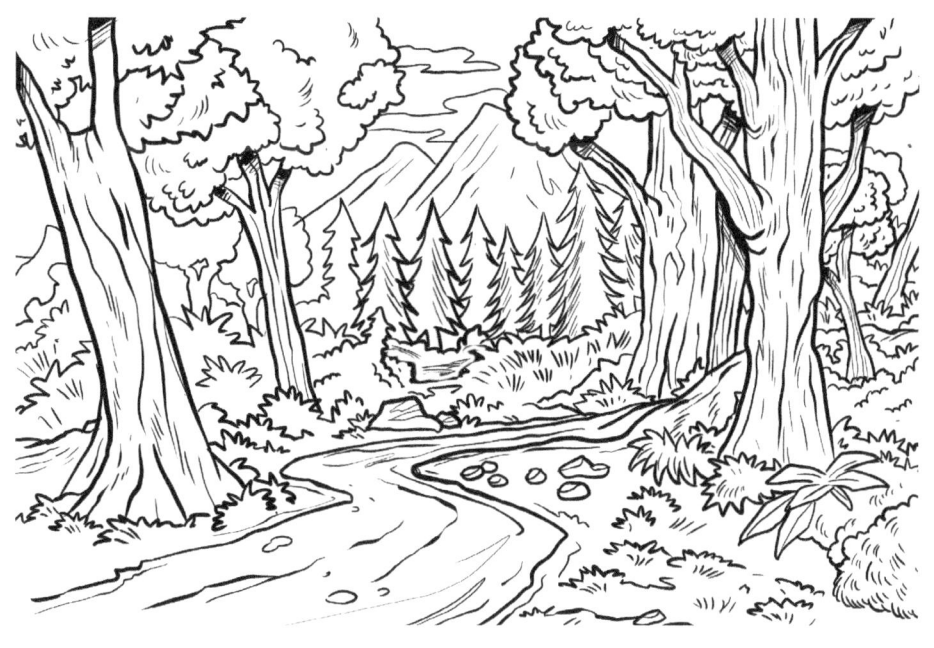
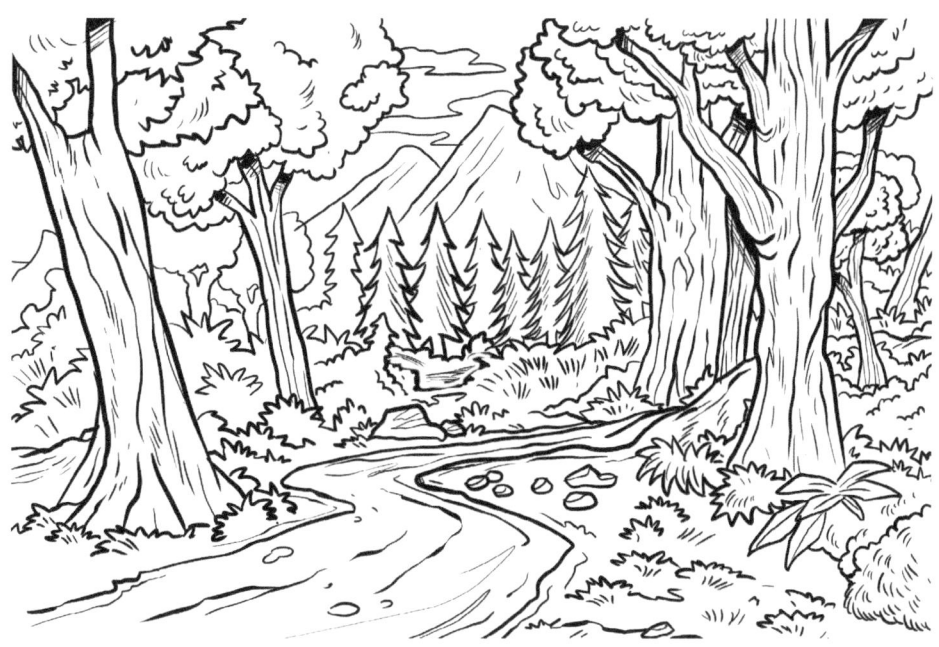

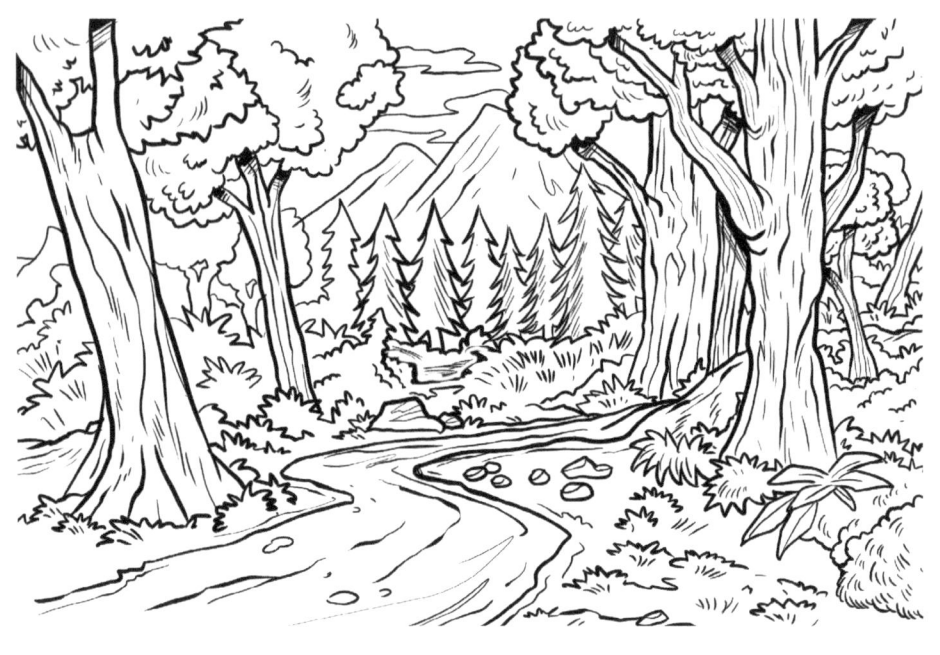
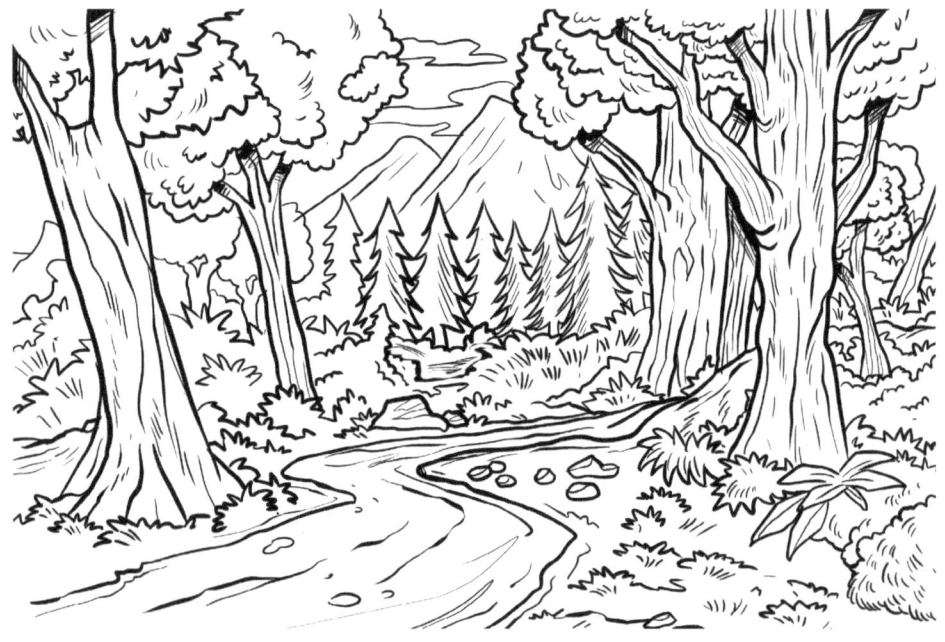

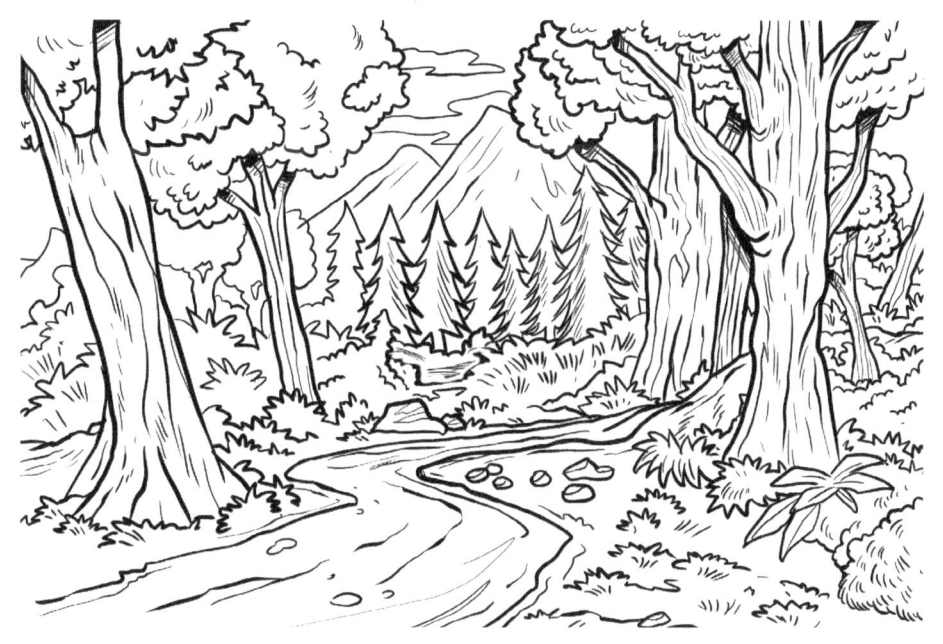
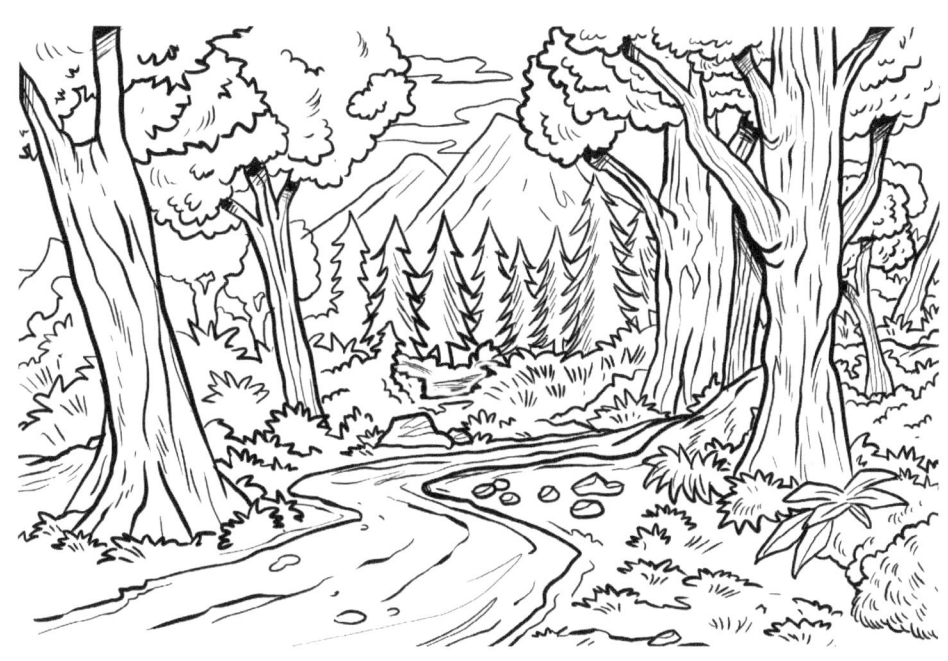

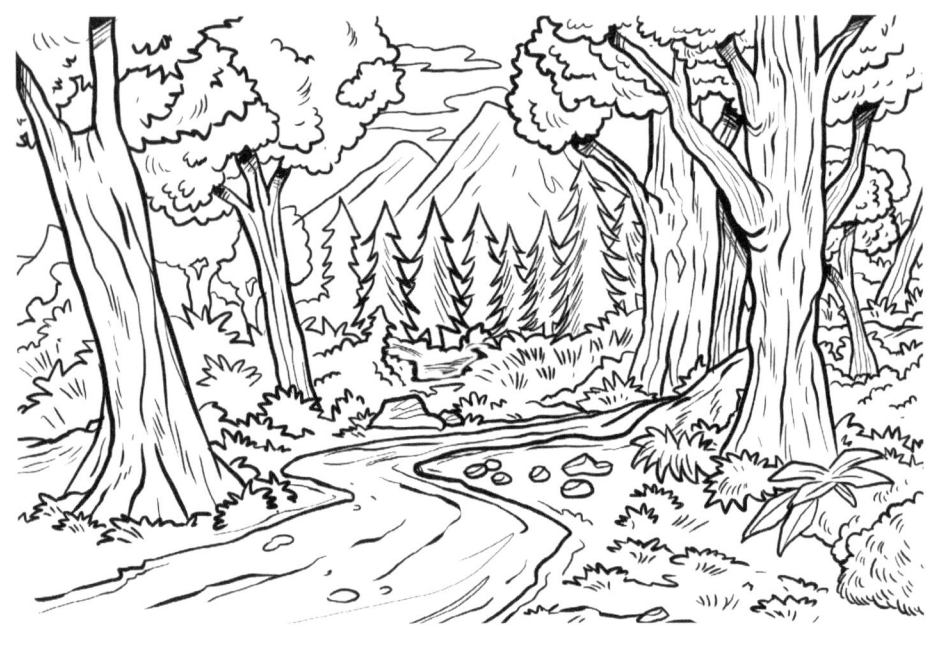

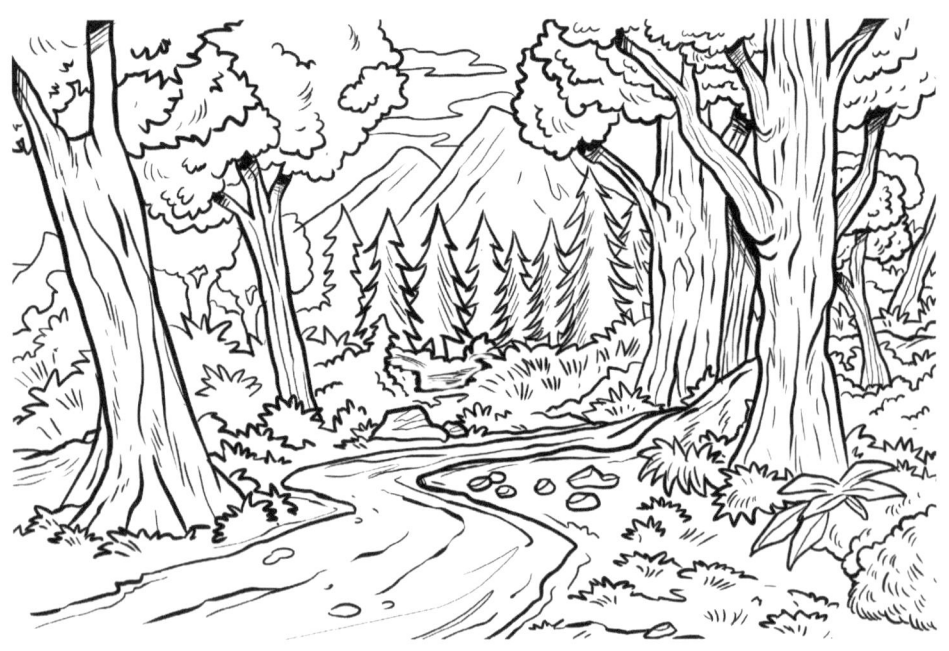

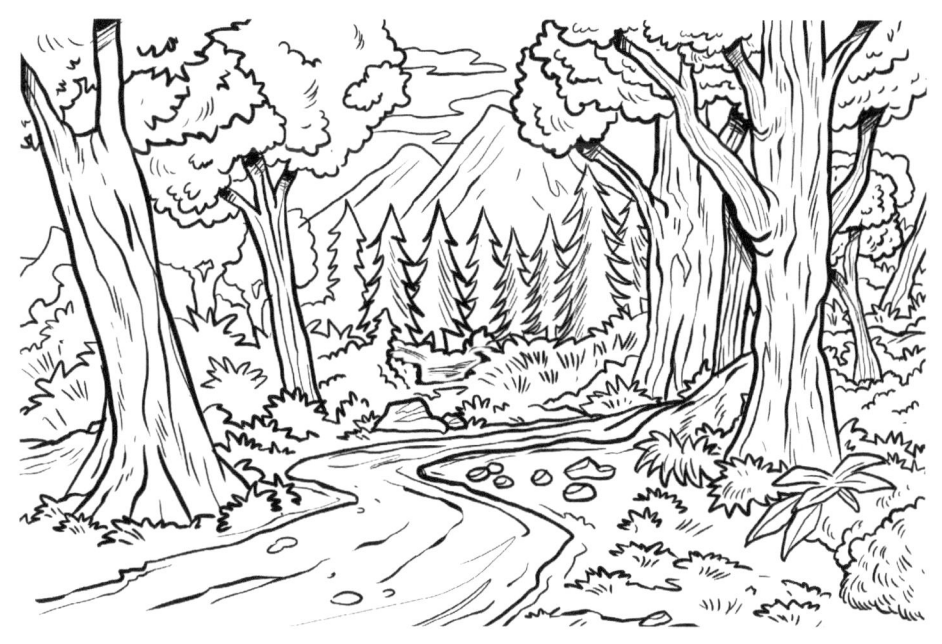
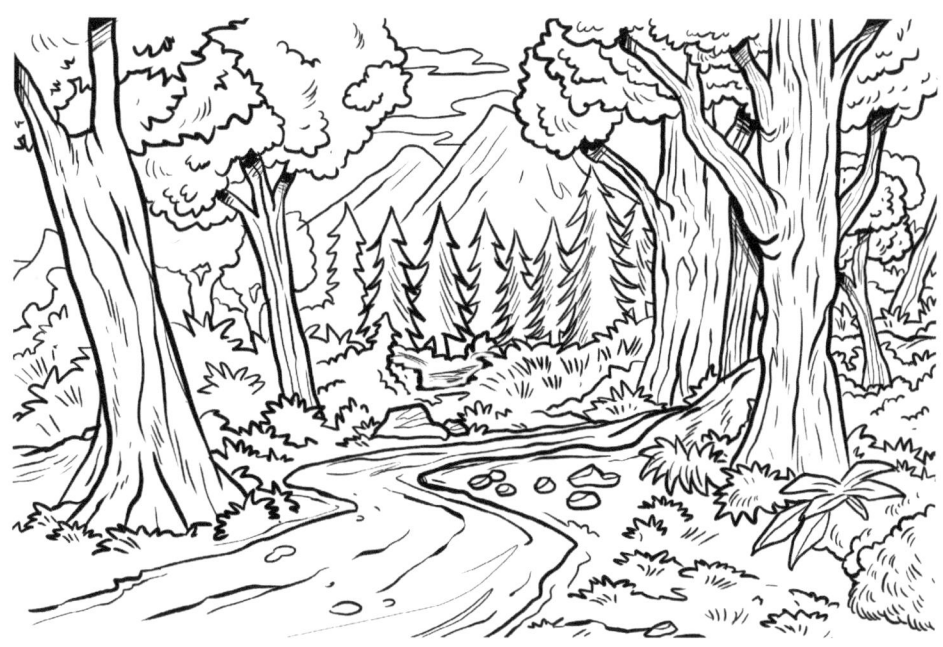

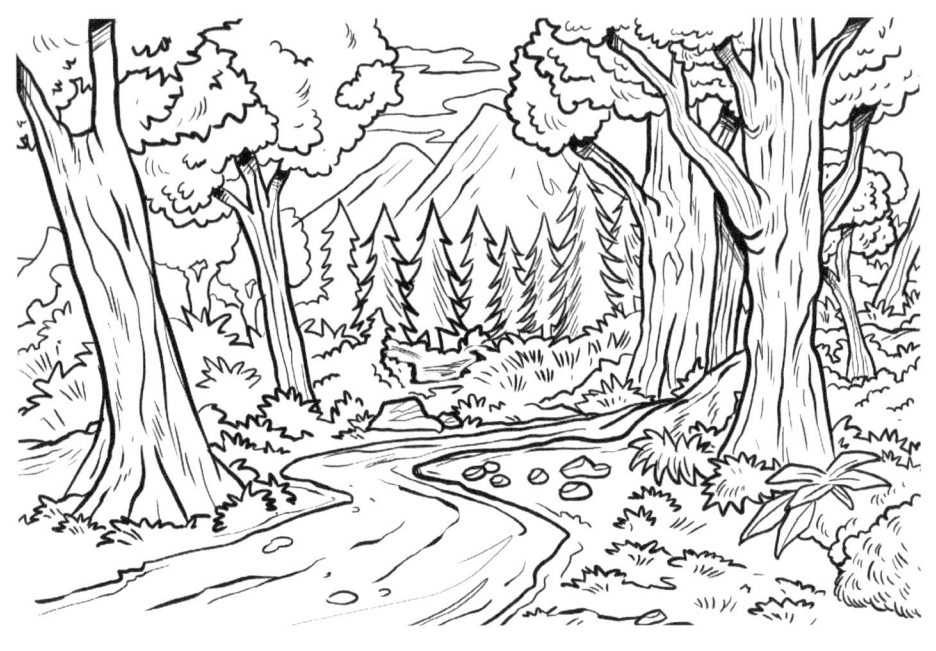
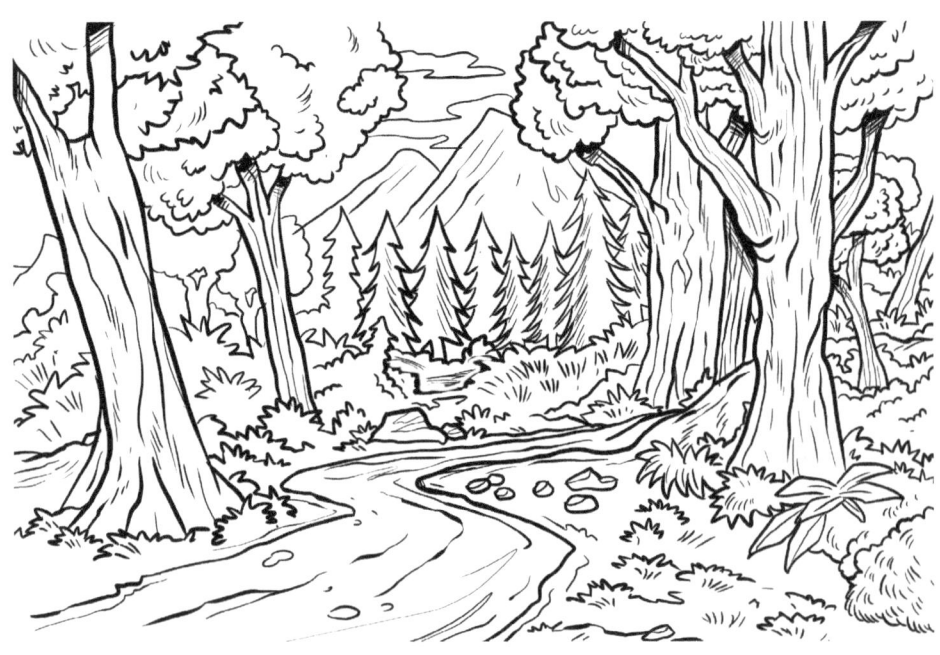

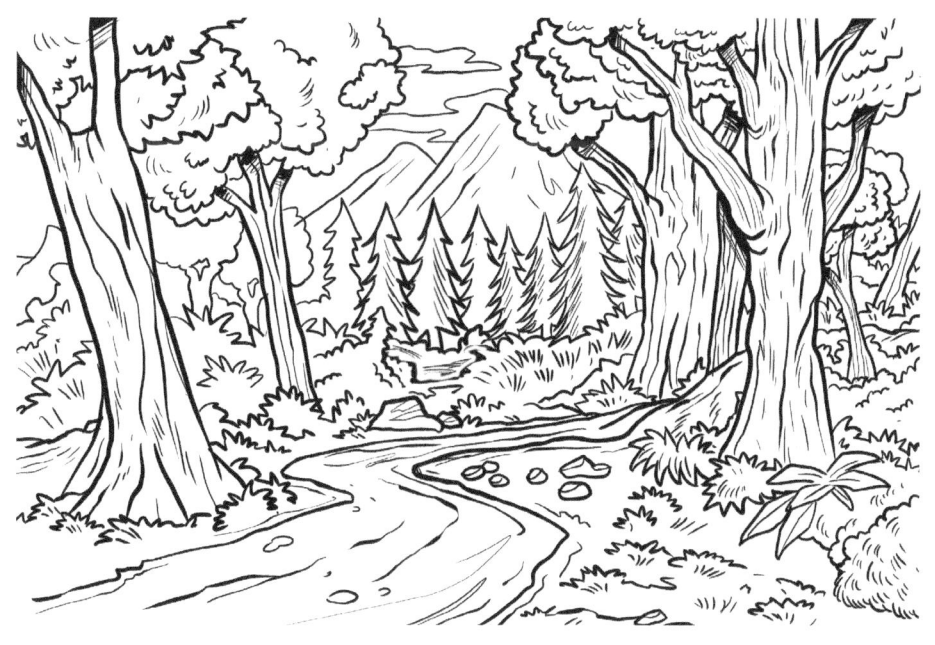
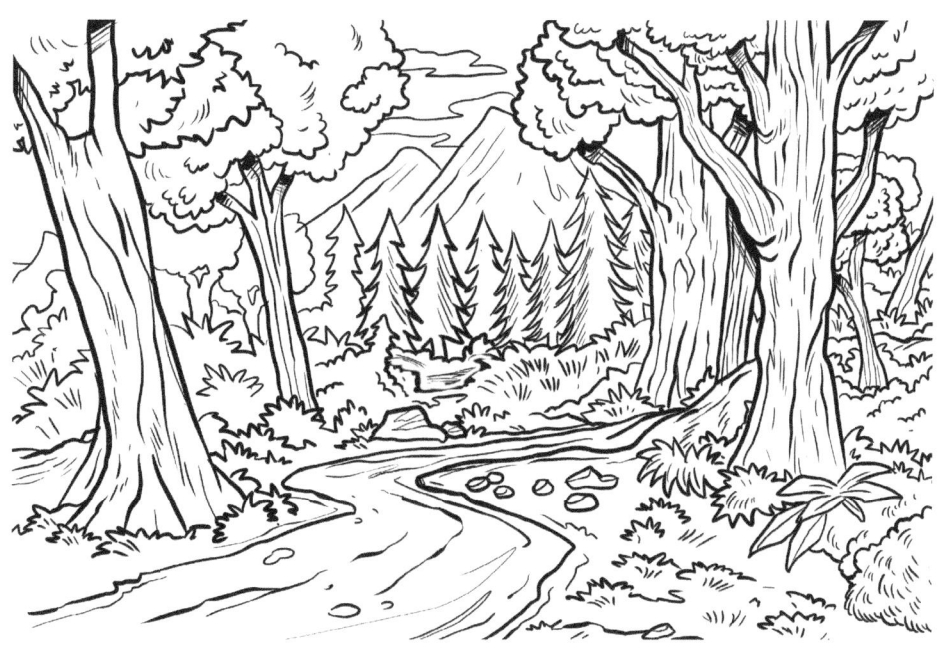

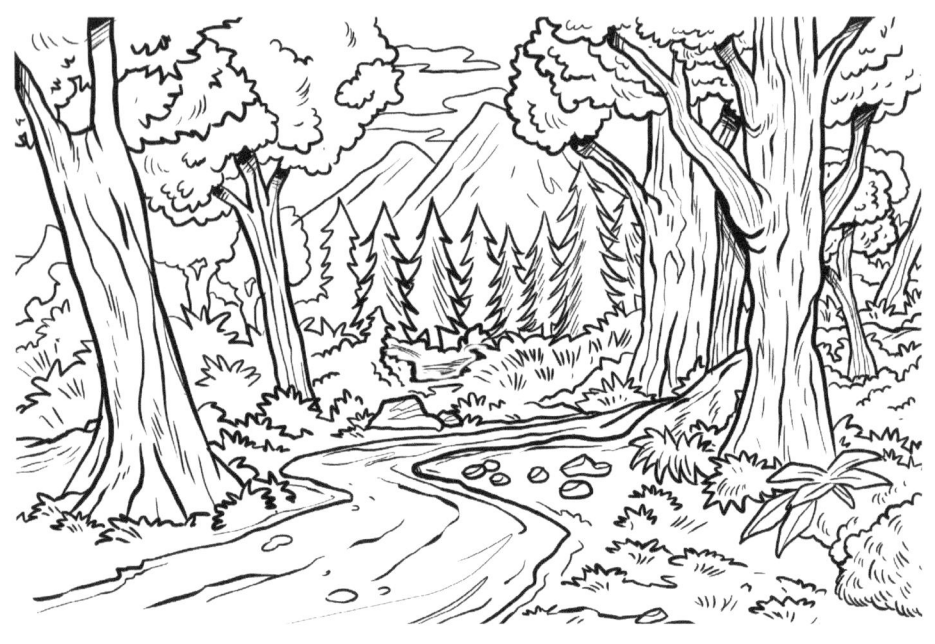
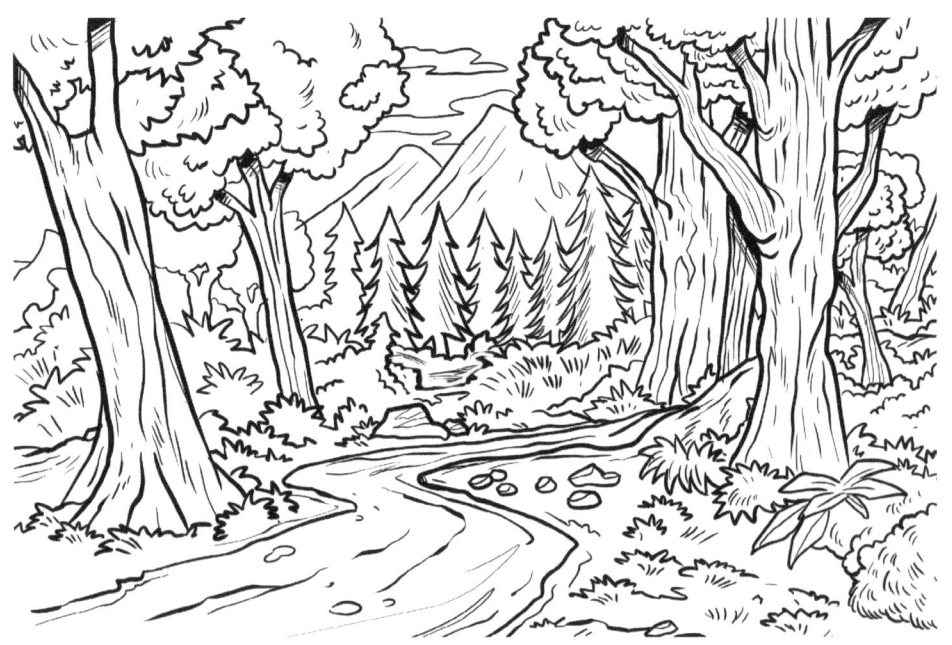

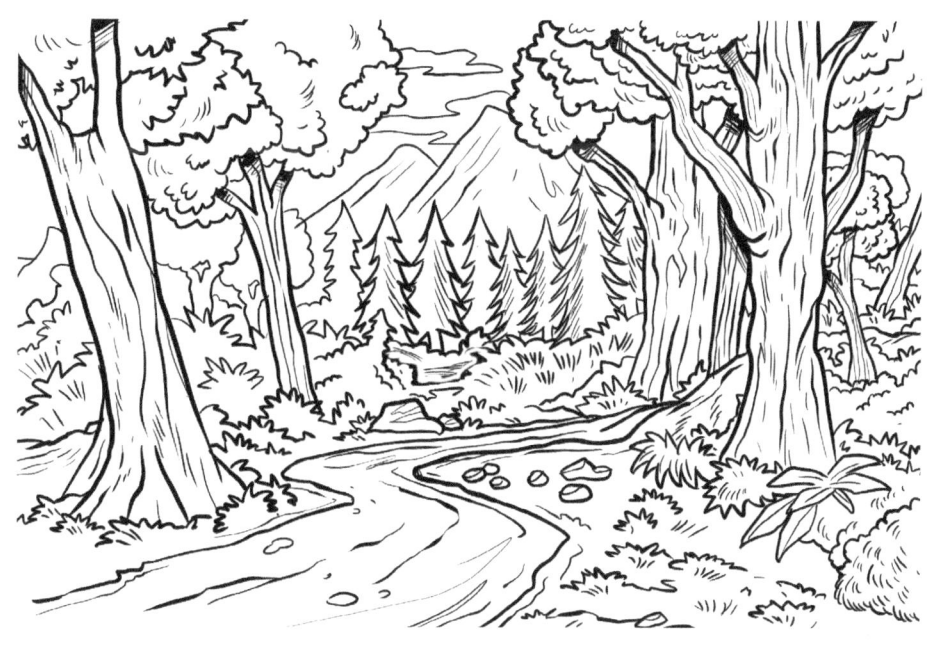
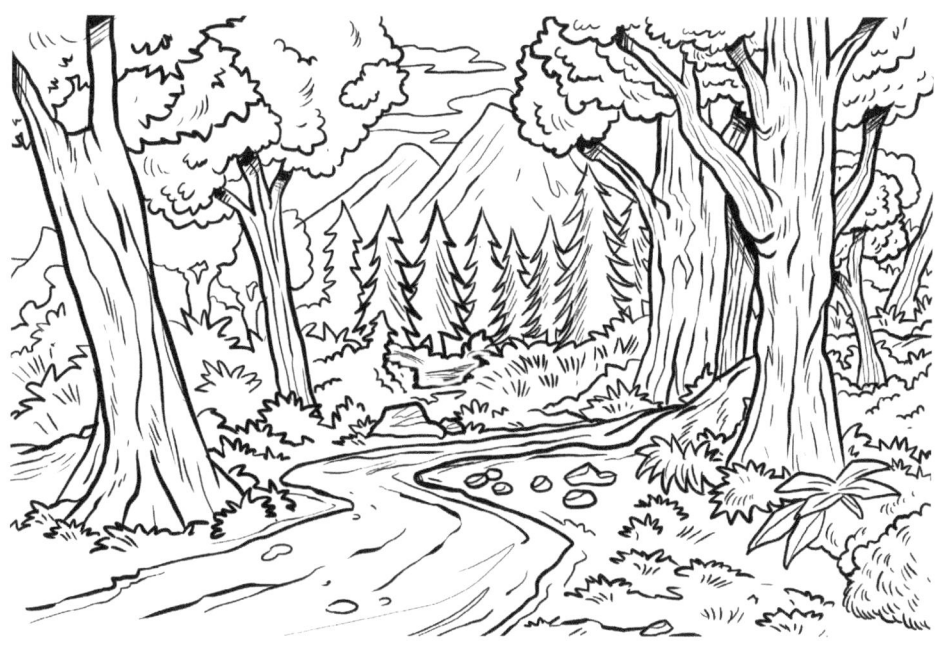

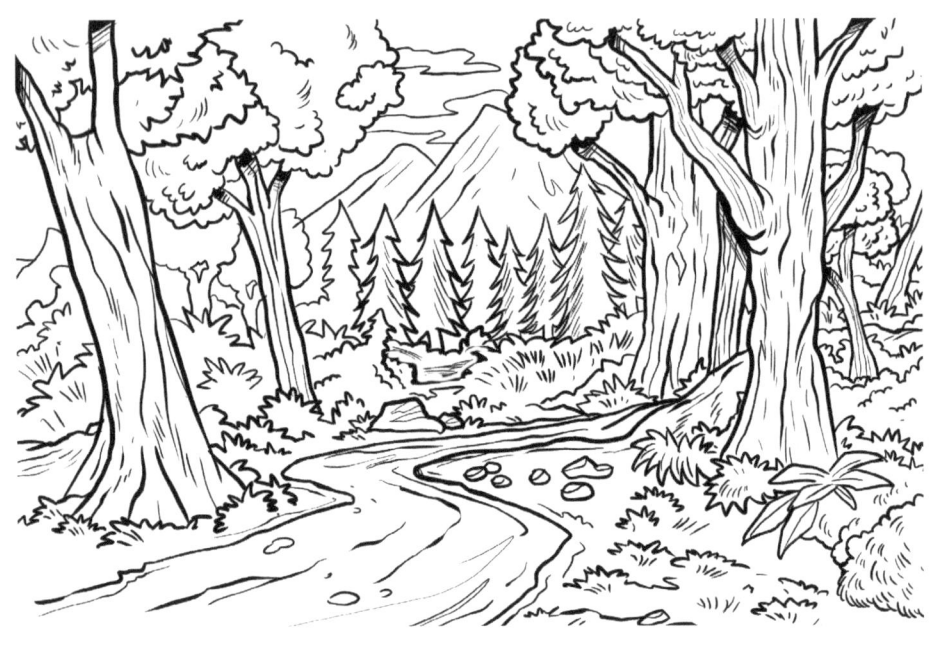
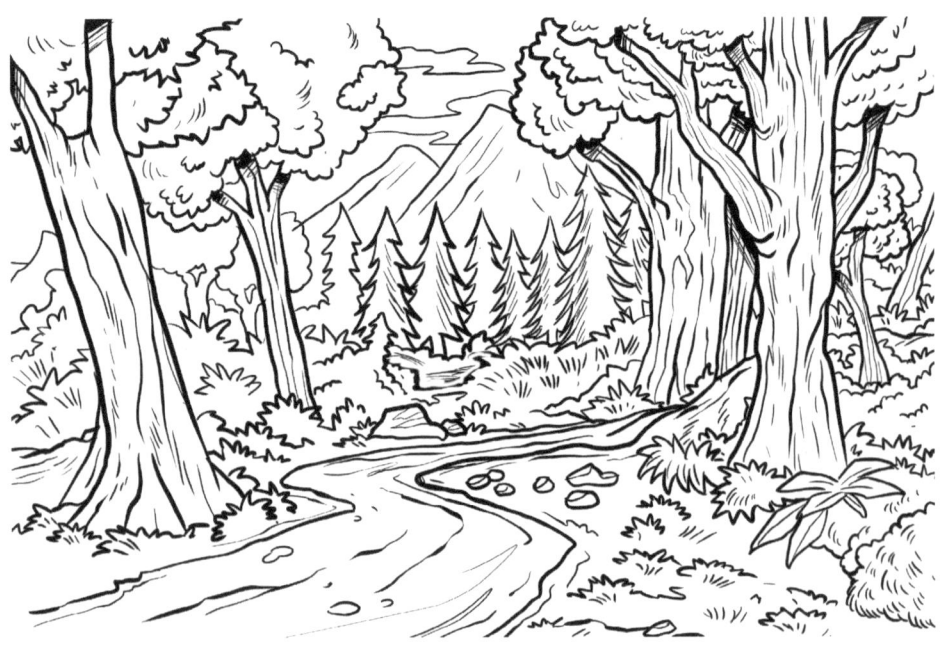

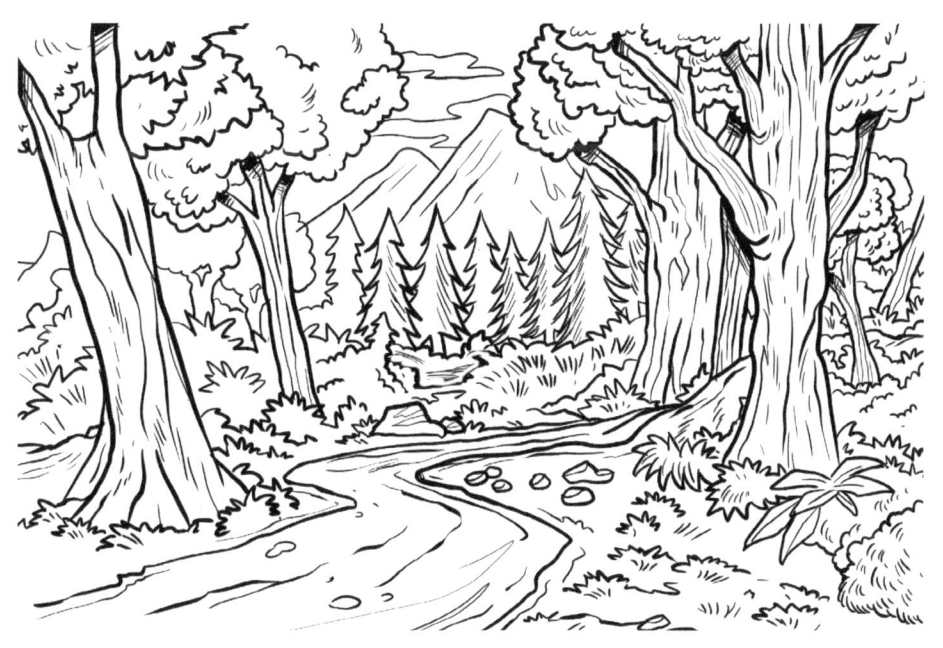
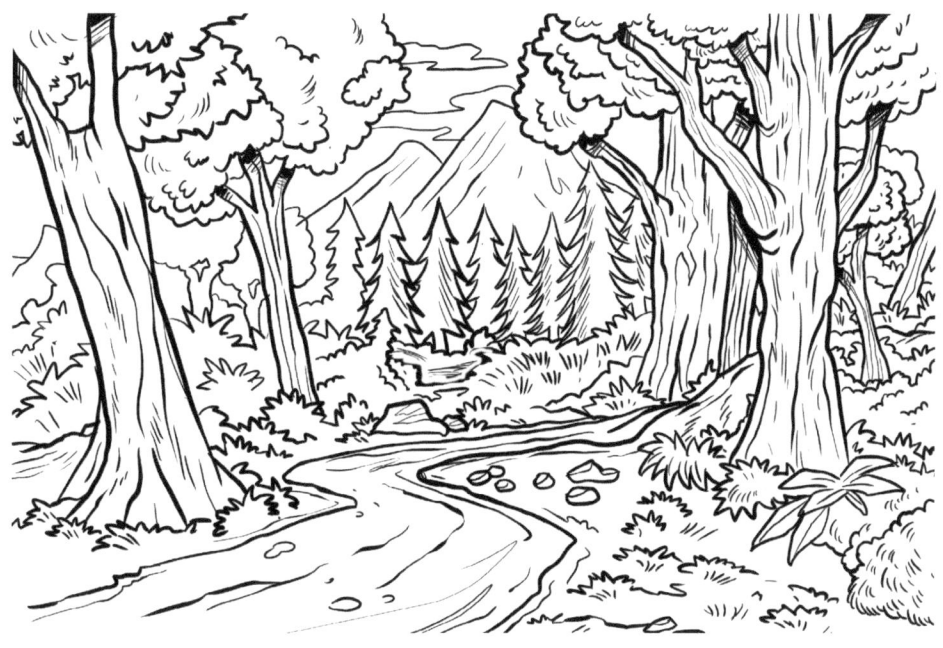

www.ingramcontent.com/pod-product-compliance
Lightning Source LLC
Chambersburg PA
CBHW040320220526
45473CB00009B/2509